Sex,
Love
And Marriage

Strengthening The Commitment
To Marriage And Family

Maurice A. Fetty

CSS Publishing Company, Inc., Lima, Ohio

SEX, LOVE AND MARRIAGE

Scripture quotations are from the *Revised Standard Version of the Bible*, copyrighted
1946, 1952 ©, 1971, 1973, by the Division of Christian Education of the National Coun-
cil of the Churches of Christ in the USA. Used by permission.

Library of Congress Cataloging-in-Publication Data

Fetty, Maurice A., 1936-
    Sex, love, and marriage: strengthening the commitment to marriage and family/
Maurice A. Fetty.
        p.   cm.
    ISBN 0-7880-1146-4 (pbk.)
    1. Sex — Religious aspects — Christianity. 2. Marriage — Religious aspects —
Christianity. 3. Family — Religious aspects — Christianity. I. Title.
BT708.F48   1998
248.4 — dc21   97-39590
                                                                                 CIP

ISBN 0-7880-1146-4   PRINTED IN U.S.A.

To Our Children

Scott, Susan, Elizabeth,

Stacy, Cynthia, Ellen

Table of Contents

Preface

One of my primary concerns in over thirty-five years of ministry has been the health and well-being of the family. Believing that human loving is a completion and fulfillment of the Divine Love, I regularly have preached sermons, taught college courses, and conducted seminars, retreats and lectureships on the topics of sex, love and marriage. It has been my goal to help people achieve the fullest possible satisfaction in human loving.

I have been privileged to perform the wedding ceremonies of hundreds of couples during my ministry. It is my hope that they have benefited from our numerous premarital counseling sessions, as I have learned from them. I have also counselled many couples in troubled marriages and relationships in an effort to help them toward a more satisfying realization of love.

Most importantly, I have attempted to elucidate some of the timeless Biblical teachings and principles to guide us in these challenging and often perplexing times. As the Source and Author of love, God is more interested than anyone in having us come into the fullness of love.

I want to express my appreciation not only for the Sacred Text and many Biblical commentators, but also for the various contemporary authorities, some of whom are cited.

But probably my own family and marriage have been the best teachers. The learning received from the faithful and thoughtful love exemplified by my parents was rudimentary. It was with my first wife, Jane Smith Fetty, who died at an early age, I first experienced the mysteries and delights of married love, and by whom we were blessed with three children, Elizabeth, Cynthia and Ellen. My wife of thirty years, the Reverend Sara A. Fetty, whose husband, the Reverend Stanley E. Melton, died at an early age, has blessed me not only with her love, insights and wisdom, but also with her three children, Scott, Susan and Stacy, and the many challenges of a blended family.

It is to *our* six children, Scott, Susan, Elizabeth, Stacy, Cynthia and Ellen, I proudly dedicate this book. Now grown and gone, some with families of their own, they bless us in more ways than we could have imagined. I hope for them the richest satisfactions in sex, love and marriage, as I do for all who might read this book.

Maurice A. Fetty

Chapter 1

Does God Think About Sex?

Then the man said,
"This at last is bone of my bones
and flesh of my flesh;
she shall be called Woman,
because she was taken out of Man."
Therefore a man leaves his father
and his mother and cleaves to his wife,
and they become one flesh.
And the man and his wife were both naked,
and were not ashamed.
— Genesis 2:23-25

It was a long-awaited survey on sex. Researchers had set out to survey American teenage boys on the question of how frequently they thought about sex. "Out of every minute, how many seconds is sex on your mind?" the researchers asked the boys.

And what was the average nationwide? American teenage boys have sex on their mind 45 seconds out of every minute! Upon hearing that, a female high school teacher was heard to remark sardonically, "And what on earth do they think about the other fifteen seconds?"

If American teenage boys have sex on the mind most of the time, so does it seem do many adult Americans. Go to any magazine rack, any bookstore, any movie theater, and in one way or another sex and sexuality are trumpeted and heralded as the all-absorbing subject.

There is hardly an American movie made that doesn't have the mandatory sex scene. Can anyone write a best-selling novel without it? And can advertisers really sell anything without using sex appeal? The fashion and publishing and entertainment industries would seem to fall flat on their face without the powerful force and appeal of sex.

And beyond the usual "normal" aspects of sexuality we have today a heightened awareness of pornography, child pornography, sadomasochism, fetishism, sexual violence and abuse, sexual harassment of women by men, and now of men by women in the popular book and movie, *Disclosure.*

Added to the usual discussions of sexuality are subjects surrounding homosexuality. Should not society and churches be accepting of same sex love? And should not practicing homosexuals be ordained to ministry and priesthood, and should there not be a provision for the sanctification of same sex marriage, so that men could live in "holy union" with men, and women live in "holy union" with women? Some denominations nationally have taken a stand to be open and affirming with respect to homosexuality. But the discussion and debate continue nevertheless.

Some years ago, while addressing questions of love and sexuality, I made mention of the "bitch goddess, success." After the service, a lady said to me, "I certainly agree with what you said about the bitch goddess (sex). I've always felt far too much importance was given to sexuality and the sexual experience. It's not as much as it's trumped up to be!" I was afraid to correct her by telling her I had said the bitch goddess "success," not "sex." I left it alone. And I said nothing to her husband!

In light of our rather compulsive obsession with the topic of sex and sexuality, we might ask ourselves again, does God ever think about sex? Edwin Johnson, in his book, *In Search of God in the Sexual Underworld*, says that there seems to be little place for God in contemporary socio-sexual realities. Indeed, in light of the morality of sexually active moderns, "traditional, moral views seem life-denying and benighted" (pp.12-13).

Johnson goes on to say that for many, sex and God have been thought to be antagonistic. In the religions, God seems to be more concerned with repressing sexual instincts than with encouraging positive and ethical attitudes toward life. Religions tend to portray God as more obsessed with governing sexual relationships than with helping people to expand consciousness and selfhood through healthy sexuality.

So how about it, does God ever think about sex? Let's take a look at the Bible, the book of God.

I.

On the one hand it must be admitted that it is difficult to find a lot in the Bible that deals explicitly with sex and sexual conduct, that is, conduct over the wide range of sexual subjects in today's almost sexually drenched world. To be sure, the Old Testament does give some explicit advice, but the Bible may not be as direct as some would like it to be. However, consider this famous passage from the book of Proverbs:

> *Three things are too wonderful for me;*
> *   four I do not understand:*
> *the way of an eagle in the sky,*
> *   the way of a serpent on a rock,*
> *the way of a ship on the high seas,*
> *   and the way of a man with a maiden.*
> — 30:18-19

I agree with the writer, the way of a man with a maiden is a mystery — a wonderful mystery.

Or consider this passage from Proverbs, the King James Version:

> *Rejoice with the wife of thy youth.*
> *Let her be as the loving hind and pleasant roe;*
> *let her breasts satisfy thee at all times;*
> *and be thou ravished always with her love.*
> — 5:18-19

And if that might seem surprising to some, even more surprising is the Bible's sensuous Song of Solomon. Here are some selected lines from that ancient wedding poem:

> *O that you would kiss me with the*
> *   kisses of your mouth!*
> *For your love is better than wine ...*

11

Behold, you are beautiful, my love,
  behold, you are beautiful!...
Your lips are like a scarlet thread,
  and your mouth is lovely...
Your breasts are like two fawns,
  twins of a gazelle,
that feed among the lilies.

These and many other passages poetically depict the beauties and wonders of sensuous love.

Does God ever think about sex? Well, where, we might ask, do you think sex came from? Just how did glands and hormones, bodies and sexual anatomy, come to be? And the answer might not be as obvious as we think, at least at first glance.

Characteristically, American popular culture has regarded religion as essentially "Puritanical" in nature, by which is meant restrictive, repressive, and coercive, with respect to human behavior, especially human sexual behavior. Sexual libertarians in America have had an ongoing crusade to overturn American Puritanical notions with respect to sexuality.

But Puritanism is much misunderstood on this subject, says historian Arthur Schlesinger, Jr. What people popularly believe is Puritanism is actually more Victorianism. And churches, until recently, have been more influenced by Victorianism than Puritanism with regard to sexuality. The Puritans actually had quite a healthy, robust attitude toward sex and love.

It was the Victorians who tended to be prudish, introverted, and extremely discreet regarding sex. Sex was attributed to the "bestial nature" of our humanity, and the "bestial nature" was most vividly expressed in the male of the species.

The females were supposedly not strongly given to such base desires and thoughts, and were set upon a pedestal to be the unsullied carriers of religion and culture and civilization. Only occasionally would they come down off their Victorian pedestal to enter the marriage bed for the necessary propagation of the race — disgusting and vulgar though it might be!

Indeed, Harvard University's famous philosopher-psychologist William James, himself a thoroughgoing Victorian, in his basic psychological work devoted only a couple of pages to sex; and even then he allowed he was a little embarrassed to bring up the subject but felt he had at least to say something about it. He reminds me of a thoroughly Victorian maiden lady in a former church of mine who was rumored to have fainted dead away in an uncontrollable swoon when I once men-tioned the word "sex" in a sermon, apparently the first time it ever was mentioned in that church!

However, the Victorians were not alone in propagating the idea that God probably doesn't think much about sex and, if so, only out of the necessity of propagating the human race. The Gnostics and Dualists and Manichaeans also had their share of influence with respect to a repressed sexuality.

And it was none other than that brilliant and seminal theological genius, Saint Augustine himself, who promulgated a kind of duality with respect to body and spirit. Please recall that in his early years in North Africa he had really sown his wild oats. He was very active sexually with a variety of women and lived with a mistress for a period of time.

Later, after going to Milan against the wishes and prayers of his mother Monica, he was converted to Christianity by Bishop Ambrose of Milan. Converted though he was, and genius though he was, he nevertheless brought with him some of his dualistic Manichaen notions. The Fall of Man, he thought erroneously, was at least partially due to sexual desire. He could not imagine Adam and Eve in Paradise being legitimately "turned on" by each other.

Consequently, for a time Augustine said, "For my soul's free-dom, I resolved not to desire, nor to seek, nor to marry a wife." And he added, "Away with the thought that there should have been any unregulated (sexual) excitement (in Paradise)...."

Does God think about sex? The Bible is a better guide than Augustine and the Victorians. Look again at the classic passages in Genesis. In the first creation story, it is God who creates the human race, male and female. He did not make us androgynous or sexless, but fully sexual, fully man and woman, with all the appro-priate glands, hormones, feelings, brains, and anatomy.

Does God think about sex? Of course. He dreamed it up, designed it, and created us as sexual beings, as passionately sexual beings. And it is as sexual beings, male and female, that we manifest the image of God. Neither maleness nor femaleness alone manifest the image of God. It takes maleness and femaleness together to do that.

Or consider the second creation story where no fit companion is found for the man so God fashions a woman around the rib of Adam. And when he awakens from the divine anesthetic he looks at her wide-eyed as she stands before him in the "altogether" and exclaims, (Wow! we might imagine): "This at last is bone of my bone, and flesh of my flesh."

You know the old feminist T-shirt which says, "God created man and then said, 'I can do better than that,' and created woman!" I agree. I like to tease my wife, saying God surely must be masculine because he made you feminine creatures so powerfully attractive!

Does God think about sex? Of course. All the time, because he created it for procreation and for deep, wonderful, rich, human companionship and ecstasy.

II.

Does God think about sex?

I asked the question indirectly to a large number of married people to whom I mailed a questionnaire. On the questionnaire I said, "Sex and sexuality receive a great deal of attention today. Should the church teach its children, youth, and adults more about sex, sexuality, and sexual relationships?"

In response to the question regarding sexuality, one mother wrote: "My children are too young to think about this. I have no opinion right now." She might agree with the story I heard the other day about two six-year-olds, a boy and a girl. She went to a Presbyterian Sunday School and he to a Baptist.

However, they were neighbors, and on a hot summer day he said to her, "Let's go swimming in my pool." "But I don't have a swimming suit," said the little girl. "That's okay," said the little boy. "We can go in our birthday suits."

So they undressed and were about to jump into the pool, but the girl stared at the boy and stared and stared and stared. Finally she said, "I didn't know there was that much difference between Presbyterians and Baptists!"

However, in response to my question "Should we teach about sex?" another person wrote, "Absolutely, but incorporate it in all the teaching subjects, particularly when the children are young. It excites so much curiosity when treated and taught as a separated subject." Another couple responded, "Yes, particularly in this age of relativism. Emphasize Christian moral standards — purity, chastity, fidelity, and LOVE, LOVE, LOVE."

Many respondents felt that sex education best belonged in the home, and if the church were involved it should emphasize the spiritual and personal aspects of sexuality as well as the physical. One man wrote, "Before sex can be taught to children, we need to redirect the instant gratification syndrome that plagues our society today." He continues, "Sex is glorious because it allows us to propagate, but it is also fun. What has to be taught is that there is a responsibility associated with sex ... love rather than lust."

A woman wrote, "Sex in church? No, not in the clinical sense — the mechanics you can get in a class or book." Then she adds, "But it would be wise to teach about sexual relationships, focusing on caring ... honor, for the total person — body, ideas, feelings; respect for the other person, always; building something together."

Another woman affirmed the church should assume responsibility in this area. She wrote, "Yes, churches should certainly have a voice in this over-discussed, 'dispirited' subject. But churches should be careful not to talk about sexual experience as an end itself. (My husband) has often observed that in this era love has become the taboo subject: everyone talks about sex, but no one talks about love."

Does God think about sex? Many would certainly affirm that he does and that at least parents, if not the church, should teach responsible sexuality. Or, as a number put it in various ways, teach that sexuality, love, personhood, and responsibility go hand in hand. Or, as the old but once popular song puts it, "Love and marriage go together like a horse and carriage." And in our view, you really shouldn't have one without the other.

While today's popular culture denies the teaching of that once popular song, the God of the Bible would not. "Does God like sex? Would Jesus be pleased with our restless urges, our fantasies, our irrational urgings for sexual experience?" asks theologian Lewis Smedes, in his fine book, *Sex For Christians.* Sexuality and all its forces and powers certainly are not denied by God and Jesus. Indeed, they are very much affirmed, but they want to keep sexuality and personhood together.

We are body persons, says Dr. Smedes. "Our sexuality always leads us beyond the physical stage to a far more personal need: we are driven inexorably into a desire for personal, intimate involvement with another person," says Dr. Smedes. He then adds, "The glandular urge, it turns out, is the undercurrent of a need for sharing ourselves with another person. Sexuality throbs within us as a movement toward relationship, intimacy, companionship" (p. 20).

Come back with me to the creation stories. The man and the woman know themselves in relation to the other because they were made for each other, not only physically, but also emotionally and psychically. The "one-fleshness" of the creation stories and the marriage vows is something more than physical. It is a shared personhood, a shared self, a shared history, and shared hopes and dreams.

It is true that out of our powerful sexual drives come some of the fiercest human passions and darkest crimes. Seduction and rape, abuse and exploitation, and now chic sadomasochism come out of our sexual stirrings. But distortions and perversions of sexual power were no more in the intent of God than distortions and perversions of any of the other powers he has given us.

Smedes affirms that "body-persons have a side to them that is wildly irrational, splendidly spontaneous and beautifully sensuous! This is not a regrettable remnant of the beast in human beings, a fiendish enemy in man's personal cold war within himself" (p. 30). Instead, it is a gift of God.

Or as Bishop Fulton Sheen once put it, "Human sexuality and love are not an ascent from the lower animals to the higher, but a descent of the divine love into human form. We are divinely created body-persons." Or as theologian Karl Barth once put it, "Our sexuality is the God-like in us." Or as Smedes says graphically, "Sexuality is a drive that begins in our glands and climaxes in communion..." (p. 33).

At this time, single, separated, and divorced people might be inquiring about themselves. Can we relate to each other as male and female without ever actually touching one another? To be sure. There is a sense in which the whole world is a kind of erotic dance between male and female, an exotic dance between masculine and feminine. And it is possible for a single person to have a full and meaningful life without being physically sexually active, as this whole dance is expressed in music and art and sociability.

What do God and teenage boys have in common? They think about sex a lot. But the difference with God is that he wants us to think of the opposite sex not just as an object for exploitation and gratification. He wants us to think of the other as a body-person, a body-person with a history, with mother and father, brothers and sisters, grandparents; a body-person in a complex web of body-persons, each throbbing with sexuality, but also each throbbing with a passion for intimacy and acceptance, affirmation and completion of identity.

Is God for us in our passionate sexuality? He certainly is. But even more, God is for us in our total body-personhood, often fulfilled in that other person, that other unique "Thou" in which we come to our true self.

Ah, yes.

> Three things are too wonderful for me;
>   four I do not understand:
> the way of an eagle in the sky,
>   the way of a serpent on a rock,
> the way of a ship on the high seas,
>   and the way of a man with a maiden.

Ah, yes, the way of a man with a maiden!
And God made it to be so!

Prayer

Loving God, Mind and Spirit of the universe who transcends all particularities of time and space, and yet chooses to embody yourself in a Son of flesh and blood in a special time and place, we thank you that you have focused yourself in Jesus, the Christ, and that in our knowledge of you, you have led us from vague ambiguities to an embodied man among men. Praise be to you.

And yet in our religious devotions, we must confess our sometime loathing of these bodies of ours. With passions and urges and impulses at times almost uncontrollable, we wonder what purity of mind and spirit might have to do with them. With the lusts of the flesh, the seductions of desire, and the enticements of the eye, we have sometimes felt that true religion meant denial of these sensate bodies and that high spirituality necessitated a low view of sexuality.

Remind us again, O Lord, that this body of ours is the result of your personal handiwork, shaped perhaps over the aeons of time. With all its passions and drives, aches and pains, beauty and glory, the body is the place of our identity, the exterior manifestation of our inward self, and you have made them both. We praise you.

Save us from body denial and body neglect. Release us from unhealthy repression of body and unwitting negation of body messages to our soul. In the name of our incarnate, embodied Lord Jesus Christ, help us to affirm ourselves as whole persons, body and soul, and to strive for health and wholeness of flesh and spirit.

We pray for our young people, so body conscious, so absorbed with powerful sex drives, so immersed in an oversexed culture. Help them to resist temptation that is only sexual, so that through chastity they might come to true love which is both body and person.

We pray for our elderly, with whom the body's aches and pains and deficiencies are uppermost. For them the spirit often is willing, but the flesh is weak. We pray for strength and the healing of their many infirmities.

And for those of us somewhere in between young and old, who may have become newly aware of our mortality in an aging body and a reflective mind, save us from the temptation to forestall our

18

mortal fears by infidelity and the greedy exploitation of others. Cause us to come to a greater maturity of self in both body and soul.

Whatever our condition, whatever our place and time in life, help us, O Lord, to be your healthy, holy people, honoring you in our bodies, which are the very temple of your Holy Spirit.

Through Jesus Christ our Lord. Amen.

Discussion Questions

1. In today's world, do you feel that churches and religion are irrelevant to the question of sexual values and behavior? In your own experience, were religious influences on the subject of sex negative, positive, or silent?

2. Should churches today introduce sex education courses at an early age? If not, why not? If so, why? Who should teach them? What should be the thrust of the church's teaching?

3. What has been your experience? Have churches been more Victorian or Puritan in their attitude toward sex? Has religion tended to think of sex as a sinful, but necessary, act?

4. In this age of considerable sexual freedom, do people feel that love and marriage go together? Are personhood and sex, soul and body easily separated in today's culture? How should the church address the question of sexual freedom and living together before marriage?

5. If sexuality is a God-given gift, should this apply also to homosexuality? Is homosexuality a gift from God? Should homosexuals be encouraged to express their sexuality in same sex partnerships or unions?

Chapter 2

Sex, Love And God

> *Do you not know that your body*
> *is a temple of the Holy Spirit*
> *within you, which you have from*
> *God? You are not your own; you*
> *were bought with a price. So*
> *glorify God in your body.*
> — 1 Corinthians 6:19-20

It is a truism to say that ours is a sex-drenched, sex-obsessed, sex-explicit culture. Pick up any newspaper, leaf through any magazine, read almost any novel, turn on almost any television show, and sooner or later the scene or conversation gets around to sex. Indeed, in one of Woody Allen's movies, he suggests early on that they go to bed together to get that over with so they can proceed to the more important matter of getting to know one another better.

As it turns out, however, according to the recent flood of publicity surrounding Woody Allen, perhaps the most important matter was sex after all. Nevertheless, celebrities everywhere boast of their sexual exploits and escapades. Even British royalty have gotten into the act with Fergie's topless bathing and Prince Charles' not-so-secret lover.

If Elvis Presley hyped the erotic urge in the fifties (and even now), no one has made more money off the sex impulse than Madonna. One of the most talented, adroit, clever, and cynical exploiters of human sexual fantasies, Madonna continues to laugh all the way to the bank as she titillates our sensual and erotic urgings. Her recent book, *Sex*, a collection of photographs of erotic poses, sells for fifty dollars and was on the best-seller list for several weeks. She is one of the most cynically clever businesswomen in American today, flaunting what she has, making us want to have it, at least in fantasy. And we pay big money for it.

But then again, there are the Amy Fishers who shoot to kill the Mary Jo Buttafuocos, the married competitors of fantasized sex. There are the Jean Harrises, former headmistress, who killed her lover of fifteen years, Dr. Tarnower of the Scarsdale Diet fame, when he jilted her for a younger woman. And there are the pathetic cases of the Sol Wachtlers, who presumably had almost everything except love, who threatens to kidnap children to get it back. And then there are spouse abusers and child abusers like John Esposito, who kidnapped ten-year-old Katie Beers, put her in his carefully designed secret dungeon and attempted to molest her sexually. What a powerful force, this eros, this sexuality, this tremendous drive for physical intimacy and personal significance.

Does God have anything to do with this powerful drive and force within us? Not very much if we follow the lead of our Victorian ancestors who regarded sexuality as somewhat bestial and beneath human dignity. But with the God of the Bible, it is quite a different story. Not only did he create us as erotic sexual beings, male and female; he intended, said Jesus, that our sexuality be expressed within the context of love and marriage, that it be the vehicle of human intimacy and communication and even an expression of the divine love.

I.

Sex, love, and marriage belong together because body and soul belong together.

We tend to separate body and soul as did ancient societies. It was precisely that problem Paul was addressing when he wrote to the Christians in Corinth, Greece. Newly liberated from the irksome legalisms of old religious laws, some Corinthian Christians used their newfound liberty for sexual license. They claimed they were free to do as they pleased with their bodies since they were under no law. Paul reminded them they were not free to exploit God's grace and to flaunt Jesus' teachings.

However, another group in the Corinthian Church was closer to the modern mood. They were the Gnostics, who, embracing an ancient dualism, regarded the world and the body as the creation of a lesser god, the god of matter as opposed to the high God of pure Spirit. Since the human soul or spirit was related to the high God, and since the body was of evil matter, decaying and dying, they reasoned that deeds done in the body had little to do with the soul or spirit. Thus it was for them perfectly permissible to have sex without love. Sex was just a physical activity and need not involve the soul or spirit at all.

Their argument is ever old and ever new. Today we are told that sex is just a natural urge or desire or appetite that should be fulfilled just as naturally as hunger or thirst. All that is needed is a cooperative and agreeable mate with whom mutual needs and appetites can be satisfied. Since sex is mostly biological and physiological, the soul or spirit or heart need not become involved. Sex can become pleasurable recreation between two agreeable mates. So the reasoning goes.

But to separate sex from the classic concept of eros and erotic life is to separate it from its driving force and its depth of meaning. Indeed, many of the so-called valueless sex education classes hardly teach the deeper meanings found in the loving sexual experience. It is a little like talking about delicious foods by describing them only as chemicals, minerals, and vitamins, rather than as wine, bread, and prime rib.

Contrary to considerable popular opinion, "sex in man is not the same as sex in animals," says Monsignor Fulton Sheen (*Peace of Soul*, p.155, quoted in *Human Nature And Christian Marriage*, W.P. Wylie, p.15). "In the animal, sex ... is a matter of stimulus and response. In man it is linked with mystery and freedom. In the animal it is only a release of tension; in man its occurrence is determined by no natural rhythm, but by the will."

Monsignor Sheen goes on to say, "(In man) ... desire is from the beginning informed with spirit, and never is one experienced apart from the other ... Sex instinct in a pig and love in a person are not the same, precisely because love is found in the will, not in the glands" (*ibid.*, p.165). Therefore the sexual acts of the body for the human are not just sexual acts; they are human acts which affect body and soul, flesh and spirit.

That body and soul are connected intimately we know well from other areas of human experience. Not long ago, a man told

23

me he had been developing an ulcer and thought he would have to have it treated medically. But then an aggravating business relationship was resolved and the ulcer went away. We know his story well, for most of us can feel the effects of stress in our bodies. And vice versa, our souls and spirits can be depressed when our bodies are ill or diseased.

Do not be deceived, says Paul. Body and soul are inextricably bound up together. If you unite your body with a prostitute, you unite your soul as well as the body. Christians are reminded that body and soul are to be kept together.

II.

Sex, love, and marriage need to be kept together because we need the sense of commitment and caring in the most intimate and tender of human relationships.

If many people today fantasize about love without marriage, others fantasize about love outside marriage. Always a part of history, the affair now seems to be standard operating procedure in popular concepts of love and marriage. It seems to be more or less expected that an affair is a part of the modern romantic fantasy and tragedy. Or as one comedienne whimsically observes, "When a husband says that he loves you so much that he thinks about you morning, noon and night, chances are that he's somebody else's husband."

Sam Keen, philosopher and author of the provocative book, *The Passionate Life: Stages of Loving*, describes his own affair after his divorce from his first wife. The woman, he says, "was twenty-seven, a romantic free spirit, a psychedelic voyager. Her mind and body were given instantly to the passing relationship. She asked no promises. Took no hostages against the future. I was 41, burdened with seriousness and trailing the chains of broken promises and a good marriage gone wrong."

Keen continues: "Yet the more we rode the edge of mounting excitement, surfed the waves of sensation, the more a mood of sullen, unspoken violence grew between us ... The ghost of the bonds we would not acknowledge returned to haunt us, until we came to hate each other for all that was missing."

Each sexual experience "reminded us," says Keen, "of abandoned and abandoning arms, days not linked to days by shared memories, too many meals eaten with strangers, broken promises, the missing center. The end has to come," says Keen. "It was time to take our separate journeys to discover how eros might be married to something abiding, whole, holy" (pp. 1-2).

In the movie *Terms of Endearment*, one of the leading characters, who is dying of cancer, is invited to visit her girlfriend in New York. After a strained luncheon with her girlfriend's three lady friends, she discovers they hardly can talk with her because she has cancer. But she blurts out to her friend that she finds it strange they cannot talk about a fatal illness because they all seem to have serious psychological and physical illnesses. One woman has a bad case of herpes (there is no good case), another has had several abortions, and the third has put her very young child in a boarding school so he will not interfere with her business and social life. Theirs was indeed a life of sex and, perhaps occasionally, love; but they were empty for lack of commitment, caring, and genuine marriage.

The Christian faith says we come to our fullest humanity in sex and love in the context of commitment and marriage. Those who have suggested that free love and uninhibited, unencumbered sex would lessen aggression and lead us to greater fulfillment have been mistaken. To be reduced to a body, to be exploited and then abandoned after sharing the most intimate of human feelings, to have been open and vulnerable, only later to be shunted aside, is indeed exploitation of the worst kind. And such rejection may well breed aggression and violence, rather than decrease them. Or it will cause us to retreat further and further into loneliness and alienation.

III.

Sex, love, and marriage are to be kept together because they are not just expressions of biological urges, but vehicles for the experience of divine love.

Monsignor Sheen put it well when he said that "love is not an evolution from the sex of the animal kingdom," but "a physiological expression of love, issuing from the Kingdom of God. Love is not an ascent from the beast, but a descent from Divinity" (*Three To Get Married*, p. 210). Eros is the vehicle for something far more profound than just the stimulation of nerve endings. It is one of the means by which humans enter into the experience of the divine love. Or as some have put it, it is the way God loves himself or the universe loves itself.

It is interesting to note how the popular understandings deny this. How often people of our time speak of doing their own thing, of finding their own ways, of indulging in the cult of narcissism. Sam Keen (*The Passionate Life*, San Francisco: Harper and Row, 1983, p. 179) says Fritz Perls' Gestalt Prayer seems to have replaced the Lord's Prayer as it reflects the new form of self-encapsulation:

> *I do my thing. You do your thing.*
> *I am not in this world to meet your expectations.*
> *You are not in this world to meet mine.*
> *If we happen to meet it is beautiful.*
> *If not, it can't be helped.*

This is similar to the Playboy philosophy which has been around for a long time. Notice it is always the play*boy* and not the play*man*; the play*girl*, and not the play*woman*, because *man* and *woman* suggest *responsibility* rather than prolonged adolescence of self-indulgence. The playboy is always so well dressed he is admired by at least two girls. He always has the perfect apartment, wears just the right cologne, and always serves just the right wine at just the right temperature. But he does not give of himself; he takes. He does not see himself as a servant or vehicle of the divine. He sees himself as the center and the girl as the object of his exploits.

And the same is true of the modern playgirl. Says Helen Gurley Brown, marriage is "only insurance for the worst years." Men are "lambs to be shorn and worn." Men are to be used, exploited, beguiled, and collected at will as sons and lovers (quoted in Keen, *op. cit.*, p. 116). And so it goes in the selfish battle of the sexes.

But that is not how God intended it. Instead, the body, says Paul, was made for the Lord, and the Lord for the body. Contradicting the libertinism and Gnosticism of his time, Paul affirmed that "the body is the spirit *incognito*" (Sandor McNab). God is not alien to the body. Instead, he has created it in his maleness and femaleness to express his divine image, to be a vehicle for his divine love.

The body, says Paul, is the temple of the Holy Spirit, the place where the presence of God dwells. God has willed that body love, eros love, be expressed between husband and wife committed to one another as God is committed to them. Thus it is in the gentle and tender love bonds of marriage the self can feel fulfilled, esteemed, and loved. Within the bonds of faithful commitment, alienation, estrangement, and loneliness can be abated and the divine union actualized. Within the marriage responsibility the body can be cherished and nourished rather than exploited and abandoned; the soul is enhanced and love is enthroned rather than profaned and banalized.

The divine love is best expressed and experienced within the commitment of marriage. Paul says that marriage union is a symbol of the mystical union and oneness of Christ and his church. The union of maleness and femaleness completes the divine love circle and provides for the ongoing procreation of life.

But sex and love outside the marriage commitment often end, as Sam Keen suggests, in hostility, regret, estrangement, alienation, loneliness, withdrawal, and sometimes violence. Read any newspaper to verify that. Those who bear the deep guilt of abortion and the terrible impediment of venereal disease or AIDS could give abundant testimony to the importance of love within the marriage bonds. On the positive side, those who have matured in love through thick and thin, who have resisted temptation and endured the trials of life and faithful love, have about them an inward beauty and God-imaged radiance that the oft-aborted, sexually careless, and emotionally selfish never quite exhibit.

In his letter to the Romans, Paul writes, "I appeal to you ... to present your bodies as a living sacrifice, holy and acceptable to God ... Do not be conformed to this world but be transformed by the renewal of your mind" (Romans 12:1-2).

And in our text, Paul reminds us, "Your body is a temple of the Holy Spirit within you ... You are not your own; you were bought with a price. So glorify God in your body" (1 Corinthians 6:19-20).

27

Our lives and bodies are not ours to do with as we please. We are to do as Christ pleases, for then we will find our truest happiness. And it pleases him that sex, love, and marriage belong together.

Prayer

Eternal God, who by the power of your Word has created the far reaches of space, and yet who has been pleased to fashion a vibrant, sensual, organic world, pulsating with life and energy, praise be to you for your creative wisdom and power. Entranced by the mystery of space and intrigued by possible life-supporting planets in distant galaxies, we are, nevertheless, repulsed by the inert wasteland of the moon and the deadly silences of the infinite void.

Having flown away in science fiction imagination to the dark boundaries of the solar system, we are drawn back to this breathing, bustling, verdant emerald-green planet of flesh and blood, and to the touch of human hands and the beholding of human eyes and the passion of human hearts. If the electronic imagination takes us into the sterile sameness of minor key wondering, we return again and again to major key triumphs of flowers in bloom and men and women in love. If the telescope and microscope presume to reveal the ultimate realities and unmask the mysteries most hidden, we would affirm today the reality of your love revealed in the suffering love of Jesus — in his salty tears and grievous wounds and blood spilled in passion for the world of sense and sound.

O God, within our deepest selves your Spirit pulsates with life organized by your Logos, your divine Wisdom and Word. You flood the world with eros love, life seeking life, stretching forward for fulfillment, standing on tiptoe for the next glimpse of throbbing ecstasy. We praise you for these gifts beyond our imaginings and yearn for the openness and courage to participate fully in all the glories you have in store for us.

We pray especially for our young people — so gifted, so vibrant, so full of energy and eros. In a day when the libertine is seen as hero and in a time when the promiscuous are upheld as role models, we pray that our young people might turn their hearts and minds to Jesus your Son, in whom we find the way, the truth, and the life. In an age that would exploit the divine potencies of sex for selfish satisfaction or impersonal profit, we pray for wisdom to understand your purposes and for the courage and strength to complete your love in our sexuality and commitment. Save us from the deceptions and delusions which bring us to emotional ruin. Guard us from the temptations which would degrade our bodies and destroy our spirits.

O divine and loving Father, grant that we may be open to your love and thus complete the circle of love with you and one another.

In Christ's name we pray. Amen.

Discussion Questions

1. Commitment seems to be difficult for many people today, especially when it comes to marriage. Is the promise of commitment for life too much to ask of people? Is it realistic? Since people change, should religious people think it reasonable to change marriage partners along the way?

2. Theologian Daniel Day Williams has suggested that human sexual loving is, in a sense, a completion of the divine love, where the masculine and feminine aspects of God's image are joined. Do the people of today feel that way about human loving? Do Christians? Should they? What do you think?

3. Many people say that their body is theirs to do with as they please. Do Christians and religious people of today feel that way about their bodies? Is Paul's idea of the body as the temple of God idealistic and unrealistic? How should Christians of today think about their bodies?

Chapter 3

A Two-Part Invention

> *Then the man said,*
> *"This at last is bone of my bones*
> *and flesh of my flesh;*
> *she shall be called Woman,*
> *because she was taken out of Man."*
> *Therefore a man leaves his father*
> *and his mother and cleaves to his wife,*
> *and they become one flesh.*
>
> — Genesis 2:23-24

I have not seen many of them lately. When I did see them a few years ago I was amused and curious. Tempted to go into one, I never did. And then the other day I came across one again. They are rarer now than in the '60s and '70s. I am speaking of the unisex hair salons. If I had my hair done there, I was never quite sure how I would come out.

If in our time unisex hair salons meant they cut both women's and men's hair and that they fashion men and women to look more like one another, the unisex idea has ancient mythological roots. Some myths suggest humans were first androgynous, that is, male-female beings in one person, and that when they became separated, they had a deep longing to be united again. It has been suggested that this longing is the origin of sexual desire.

Some scholars have suggested there is a hint of this idea in one of our biblical creation stories. In it, God takes a rib from the man and fashions a woman around it. It is as if the female sexuality is the male sexuality turned outside in. Because they come out of one being, to become two, they have a longing to overcome the separation, to become one again. That longing is manifested in sexual desire.

However, the other biblical creation story found in Genesis, chapter one, is a little different. In that one, man is not created first and then woman out of man. Instead, they are created at the same time. As the Bible puts it:

> *Then God said, "Let us make man in our image, after our likeness; and let them have dominion ..." So God created man in his own image, in the image of God he created him; male and female he created them. And God blessed them, and God said to them, "Be fruitful and multiply, and fill the earth and subdue it; and have dominion ..."*
> — Genesis 1:26-28

In this story the sexes are differentiated from the very beginning, rather than being pulled apart into male and female or the one coming out of the other. Notice that humankind is created in the image of God as male and female, masculine and feminine. When God chose to express himself in human form, he did so sexually in both genders. Both maleness and femaleness express the image of God. Both masculine and feminine manifest what God is like.

Note that contrary to latter-day interpretations of the fall of man in the Garden of Eden, sexuality is not sin. Quite the contrary in the first story. Sexuality is intended as the vehicle by which the living creatures of the earth are to multiply themselves, including human beings. Rather than creating from nothing each time as at the beginning, God gave to creation itself the gift of procreation — the power to continue the miracle of new life by cooperating with the reproductive powers given by God.

Of course, Roman Catholics have tended to favor this creation story over the other, believing the basic reason for sexuality to be that of procreation. Some Protestants have embraced similar views. However, many Protestants and others have emphasized the other story, pointing out that Adam was lonely and in need of companionship with a being like himself, yet different. To meet Adam's need God did not first create another man, but a woman.

In this story, woman is the means by which a man comes to himself, and man the means by which a woman comes to herself.

Sexuality is not provided just to "be fruitful and multiply." It is designed by God for fulfillment, communication, and companionship. Indeed, the very word "helpmate" implies in Hebrew "answerer." A woman was one who, unlike the animals, could answer in human language. Man and woman were made for communication with each other sexually, psychologically, and spiritually.

Together they satisfy the deep human longing for oneness, for harmony, for integration, for belonging. They are indeed, in Madeleine L'Engle's words, "a two-part invention," each part needing and complementing the other. Like the keyboard pieces by Bach, they together make divine music and express the divine image in the world. The masculine and feminine provide a divine dance, a divine two-step with which the world is blessed and by which it is fulfilled.

But the two-part invention is troubled in our time, especially as it relates to marriage and masculine/feminine relationships. The scriptures have good advice on how to improve the invention and to move it toward the designs God had in mind.

I.

In our ancient text we are advised that because a man and a woman were designed to be together, *a man leaves his father and mother ...*

In the traditional wedding ceremony the opening address quotes those very words, that "a man shall leave his father and mother...." It should also say a woman shall leave her father and mother, but the ancient scriptures do not mention that, nor did Jesus when he quoted this passage from Genesis.

In my premarital counseling with couples over the years I often have pointed out the importance of "leaving home" or "leaving father and mother," or in the case of a second marriage, of really leaving the ex-wife or ex-husband.

One divorced man told me he was so grateful his second wife had the same name as the first, that way he could be sure he would never slip up and call her by the wrong name! He was wise enough to know that previously married people often have a hard time moving beyond the previous marriage. They tend to place the

33

second spouse in the same niche or slot as the first spouse, even calling him or her by the former spouse's name. Thus the two-part invention becomes a three- or four-part invention if we drag former partners into the divine dance of love. People getting married for the second or third time have to leave the past behind to move on to a new, creative future.

A woman at a cocktail party seemed to have that in mind when she approached a man and said, "You look like my third husband." He asked, "How many husbands have you had?" She said, "Two." She realized she needed to leave the past to move on to a new future.

So do people getting married for the first time. When I suggest to couples the importance of leaving home they sometimes wince a little because they perceive themselves as already having left home. They may be living miles from parents and often are in fact living together. Yet leaving home is more subtle than geographical distance.

Some years ago friends of mine were having marital problems. They went to a psychiatrist who eventually advised my friend that he was too attached to his mother, too dependent on her. His wife agreed.

"How can that be?" my friend exclaimed. "My mother lives 600 miles away." His wife complained that that meant nothing. Any time he had an important decision to make affecting their personal lives, he would call his mother and together they would decide and tell his wife. His wife rightly complained that she was excluded, that he was still tied to this mother's apron strings. They're divorced now.

A man in marital counseling complained about his wife and her imposition of her family traditions upon him. "Whatever we did in our marriage had to be a copy of what her parents did in their marriage and family," he said. "We had to celebrate Christmas, Easter, and Thanksgiving the way they celebrated it. We had to open presents on Christmas Eve as they did rather than on Christmas morning as we did. We even had to have the same foods they had." Obviously, this man was complaining about a woman who refused to leave father and mother.

The two-part invention is designed for risk. It requires the risk of vulnerability, the risk of going out toward the other, the risk of taking a chance on leaving our security for the thrill of meeting and the ecstasy of love. Many of us, living in fear, cling unduly to the securities of the past. We are perpetual wallflowers on the sidelines of the divine dance God intends for us.

Fortunately, we are impelled and drawn by the powerful forces of masculinity and femininity. Fortunately, we have the lure of sexuality and the assurance that he or she is bone of my bone, flesh of my flesh.

Nonetheless, we must leave the security of father and mother behind in the adventure of risking and meeting, in the divine dance of loving and procreating. The family name we own as children, the family identity we enjoy from a common mother and father, was itself the product of a man and woman leaving the security of father and mother to develop a new unit of love to celebrate fulfillment and procreation.

II.

If the ancient biblical text says man should *leave* his father and mother, it also says he should *cleave* unto his wife, and they become one flesh.

The word "cleave" appears in our traditional wedding ceremony and we use it advisedly. Some revised ceremonies substitute "be joined together" for "cleave." For us "to cleave" can mean to separate, to split apart as does a meat cleaver in the butcher shop. A "cleavage" suggests a separation rather than a coming together. As Prince Philip remarked to Dolly Parton when meeting her with a low-cut gown: "My father told me that when I met a woman dressed like you, I should look her directly in the eye!"

But in this ancient text quoted and affirmed by Jesus, "to cleave" means to come together in such a way as to be one flesh. Male and female were designed for each other and meant for each other. Maleness and femaleness are not bad or dirty or bestial. Our sexuality is not the result of the fall of man from paradise nor is it to be thought of as degrading or disgusting. Instead, our bodies, genitalia and all, are part of the earthly expression of God's being and power and person.

Maleness and femaleness are categories defined primarily by anatomy. But masculinity and femininity are broader, more inclusive concepts. The famous psychiatrist Carl Jung believed we have both qualities within us. Men have a feminine as well as a masculine dimension. And women have a masculine as well as a feminine dimension.

The coming together as masculine and feminine is much more complex and rich than coming together merely as male and female. This may explain some of the allure for people of the same sex. The masculine and feminine in each seems to draw them toward each other despite their outward sexual definition.

The masculine-feminine goes deeper than that — perhaps to the heart of the universe itself — to God. Possibly the whole universe is a divine dance, a pulsation back and forth, up and down, together and apart in an infinite creative process toward harmony and growth. Our music and art, athletics and literature, commerce and religion may all reflect the dynamics of the masculine-feminine powers implicit in all creation. In that sense, married or single, we can participate in the divine dance of masculine-feminine.

But the focus for us today is on the two-part invention having to do with heterosexual love and marriage. In that relationship, there is to be not only a leaving, but a cleaving; not only a coming apart from the one flesh or father or mother, but a coming together to be one flesh with our spouse. Our leaving is not for the purpose of license or libertinism, but for linkage with that one other in whom we know and are known.

In her book *The Irrational Season*, Madeleine L'Engle says that "to marry is the biggest risk in human relations that a person can take" (p. 47). But in a trial marriage or a short-term commitment, "we don't have to risk ourselves; we can hold back" (*ibid.*).

Ms. L'Engle goes on to point out that commitment to one person "is not, as many people think, a rejection of freedom; rather it demands the courage to move into all the risk of freedom and the risk of love which is permanent, into that love which is not possession, but participation" (*ibid.*).

Like a Bach fugue, love-making cannot be learned all at once. Love based solely on the "combustion of two attracting chemistries tends to fizzle out," says L'Engle. "A long-term satisfying marriage moves beyond chemistry to compatibility, to friendship and to companionship" (*Two-Part Invention*, p. 76). L'Engle knew what she was talking about from her own beautiful, long marriage to her actor-husband Hugh Franklin.

She recalls telling a New York taxi driver that she and her husband were celebrating their thirtieth anniversary. She remarked that she thought it somewhat of a record, inasmuch as her husband was an actor and she a writer. The taxi driver looked back at her and said, "Lady, that's not a record, that's a miracle."

Theirs was not a love that grew in a straight line, but "a series of hills and valleys." She and Hugh as well as most of us in our marriages know love is like that — some desert places between the lush, green, satisfying oases of ecstasy and contentment.

L'Engle maintains it is important to remain a self in marriage, and not to subsume oneself into the other so as to lose identity. We sometimes use a unity candle in wedding ceremonies today. It consists of three candles on the altar. The two outside candles are lit before the ceremony, and then after they are pronounced husband and wife, the bride and groom light the center candle to symbolize their union. In the old days they used to blow out the side candles to symbolize the merger of their total identity. But not today. Most leave the side candles lighted to symbolize their individuality, as well as their marriage.

Marriage is a two-part invention, a divine dance of male-female, masculine-feminine. By the same token, we have to accept the partner for who he or she really is, instead of expecting that person to be the image we wanted to marry.

To be sure, there are many today who ask, why marry? Allan Bloom in his book, *The Closing of the American Mind*, observes that "one of the strongest, oldest motives for marriage is no longer operative. Men can now enjoy the sex that previously could only be had in marriage" (p. 132). And, says Bloom, young people are afraid of making commitments. Yet love *is* commitment, says Bloom, "commitment and much more" (p. 122).

Theologian Daniel Day Williams agrees. Sexuality is not an end in itself, but a way of seeking another, a way of being joined to another in communication, companionship, and commitment. The implicit question in all human sexual attraction is, says Williams, "What do you want and expect from me? What use will you make of me? And are you exploiting me or loving me?" (*The Spirit and the Forms of Love*, p. 221). Indeed, our selfhood is bound up in our body and sexuality. And it is the will of God that masculine-feminine, male-female, be joined together in love to become truly one flesh.

It's a two-part invention — our maleness-femaleness, masculinity-femininity — a two-part invention expressing the very nature of the Divine Inventor himself. May God help us in our leaving and our cleaving to be truly joined to each other to be one flesh in our marriages.

Prayer

Eternal God, who has within your Being all the powers of the universe, and who has manifested yourself to us as Person within the context of the earth and human history, we praise you as the Source of our being and worship you as the Creator of all that is.

God of all time and space, who lures the galaxies into being and who knows the stars by name, so that all the morning stars sing together and your sons and daughters dance for you, forgive us if at times we feel you have neglected us or have grown indifferent to our human drama. As your power is exhibited in the forces of the universe, remind us of the powers you have placed within each of us — powers of thought and will, faith and love and procreation.

In your holy and powerful presence where love and creativity never cease, it is for us to confess our fearfulness and defensiveness. Called to play in the divine orchestra of living and loving, we have been reluctant to share our talents and our selves. Demanding only the solo passages and starring performances, we have not been willing to give our gifts in love for the good of the whole. Help us always to be willing to give rather than always being anxious to receive. Forgive us where we fall short of your expectations for us.

Creator of us all, you have been pleased to focus yourself in the human image, male and female, masculine and feminine. What awesome powers you have placed within us. How violent we can become with passion in our search for acceptance and significance.

We especially pray for our young people as they come into adolescence. We parents, churches, and schools confess how inadequate we have been in our teaching of sexuality and morals. Uncomfortable ourselves talking about these powerful forces within, we have neglected talking to our young in meaningful ways. Help us all to come to greater enlightenment and to assume more responsibility to help our young people in creative and relevant ways.

We pray for our youth, that they will have the strength to resist sexual temptation which exploits and degrades. Lead them to companions and friends who build up their personhood rather than tear it down. Grant that theirs eventually may be the joy of celebrating masculinity and femininity in the adventure of committed marriage.

And for those of us along in years, we pray your blessing. For those long married and a little bored with each other, we ask for eyes opened to see all the hidden potential in the other for something new. For those in troubled marriages, we ask for new insights into the self and the relationship and a new empowerment to bring them to the joy you intend for them. For the widowed, we pray healing for the grief and wisdom in choosing a new mate, should that be their desire. And for the divorced, we ask healing of the pain and release from the anger so as to be able to go on to build a new life and love.

O Eternal God, progenitor of us all, grant us strength to use wisely our powers of eros and sexuality, so that we may come to the wholeness and joy you intended for us from the beginning of creation.

In the name of Christ we pray. Amen.

Discussion Questions

1. Some Christians believe the sexual experience is only for pro-creation and not just enjoyment. Is sexual experience for enjoyment legitimate? Why? Why not?

2. It often is said that we do not marry an individual, we marry the individual and his or her family with all the hereditary traits, strengths, weaknesses, and idiosyncracies. If a prospective bride or groom has low regard for the prospective partner's family, should they marry? Will not the partner be like the family? What should a partner do if he or she is already married into a family for which he or she has disregard?

3. Is Carl Jung correct when he asserts that men have a feminine dimension and women have a masculine dimension? Do you know people who would seem to exemplify his idea? Do you experience the opposite dimension within yourself? How might couples blend these dimensions in a satisfactory way?

4. Should married couples today think of themselves as one, or should they strive to keep their separate identity and individuality? In which areas should couples strive to be one, and in which areas should they strive to be separate and individual?

Chapter 4

How To Love Men

Let all bitterness and wrath and anger
and clamor and slander be put away from you,
with all malice, and be kind to one another,
tenderhearted, forgiving one another,
as God in Christ forgave you.
                                    — Ephesians 4:31-32

When it first appeared it drew a few chuckles from a variety of sources. "What is this, San Francisco or something?" asked one person. "Is this the advice chapter for gay men?" queried another, upon seeing this chapter title.

No doubt the title could suggest a chapter on same sex love, and in fact we will have some things to say about men loving men. But even more we want to speak about women loving men, and about our culture in general loving men.

The subject of loving men may seem out of date or out of step with the dictates of today's political correctness police. And certain feminists and lesbians might think the topic totally irrelevant to their interests. In fact, even heterosexual women might believe the idea of loving men to be a quaint sentiment left over from a Humphrey Bogart movie.

As a matter of fact, it has become quite popular not to love men, but to hate them; not to esteem them but to belittle them; not to build them up, but to tear them down. In a recent *Newsday* feature, writer David Behrens says that "male-bashing" has now become fashionable in the popular culture. No longer able to bash blacks, Jews, Hispanics, drunks, the poor, and gays in a world where political correctness reigns, there is, says Behrens, only one suitable target left for bashing — men.

It doesn't matter who you are, he says. Young and old men, nerds and eggheads, wimps and athletes, egoists and oddballs, successful and unsuccessful — all seem to be targets of bashing. For example, back in 1988 when housewife Cindy Garner got too frustrated with her husband, she published a book titled *Everything Men Know About Women*. It sold 350,000 copies and each one of its 128 pages was blank!

She went on to publish a book titled *How Men Are Like Noodles*. Its pages were full of questions and answers like these. "What's a man's idea of helping with the housework? Lifting his legs so you can vacuum." Or this one, "Why do we need female astronauts? Because if their spaceship gets lost, at least someone will be there to ask for directions."

Hallmark greeting cards also decided to get on the male-bashing bandwagon. Says one card in its new "'let's get the guy" series, "There are easier things than finding a good man. Nailing Jell-O to a tree for instance." Substitute the name of any minority in this or any other male-bashing card or book or joke, and you will see how "in" and how callous male-bashing has become in some sectors.

In the basher's manual, there is easy justification, says Behrens. In their thinking men have been brutish, insensitive, dirty-mouthed, and rape-minded for so long that they deserve all the bashing they get. Typical of biased people, the bashers stereotype and generalize to justify their hostility toward a particular group. If in the past it was the Jew, the black, the Pole, the Jap, or the WASP, now it is the male of the species. And so the age-old war between the sexes has taken on a new and somewhat vicious dimension.

But in the church, our concern is not with bashing, but with loving. We are more interested in construction than destruction, more ardent for reconciliation than revenge, more determined for peace in place of warfare, and more concerned to promote the ecstasies available between the sexes than the agonies.

How then might we improve our love for men?

I.

For one thing — and this may sound strange — *men need to learn to love themselves.*

We have had a new rash of violence in our country. Drive-by shootings seem almost commonplace. Schoolchildren are so frightened for their safety, some of them now even speak of planning their own funerals. Mass killings in restaurants have grabbed the headlines. Long Island was jolted with the discovery of the Joel Rifkin serial killings and the hate-crazed killings and maimings on the Long Island Railroad. And the perpetrators of these horrendous crimes were men. Indeed, the vast majority of perpetrators of violent crimes are men.

There are many reasons for this, of course. Men have been physically stronger than women, and thus more able to carry out violent crime. But most of the victims of violent crime are men of the same race. Frustrations of poverty, injustice, and rejection can lead many to violence. Perhaps most of all, it is a sense of powerlessness that frustrates many men.

This may sound strange to some feminists who seem to presume that once they have equal rights to men, they will somehow be imbued with power. That may be true if a *New Yorker* cartoon comes true. It shows a feminist yuppie attired in blouse, jacket and tie, and sneakers standing before the huge desk of the cigar-smoking corporate chief. She says, "Please, sir, I want it all — now!"

For most everyone else — men included — the all doesn't come — not now or ever. Indeed, one of the powerful elements of most men's mid-life crises is just that — the realization of how relatively powerless they are. Not only do they begin to see they will never rise to the top of the corporate pyramid or become the famous and rich trial lawyer or publish the great American novel; not only do they see that, they also see their mortality. No matter how they might try to bolster their youthfulness with a new convertible or an affair or physical fitness program, the relative powerlessness of their life settles in as densely as a New England fog.

Arthur Schlesinger, Jr., has written that "no social emotion is more widespread today than the conviction of personal powerlessness, the sense of being beset, beleaguered, and persecuted" (quoted in *Power and Innocence*, by Rollo May, p. 21). Indeed, few of us feel we can affect government or business, school or church or even our own family in significant ways.

Strangely enough, it is out of our sense of impotence and powerlessness that our violent emotions often merge. "It is important

43

to see," says psychoanalyst Rollo May, "that the violence is the end result of repressed anger and rage, combined with constant fear based on ... powerlessness" (*ibid.*, p. 26). He goes on to add that, strangely, violence is a way of building a sense of self-esteem and significance. Indeed, who knew the names of Lee Harvey Oswald or Charles Manson or Joel Rifkin or Colin Ferguson before they committed their murders?

But men, we need to learn to love ourselves, to accept ourselves, to nurture ourselves. I'm not speaking here of egotistical mania or narcissistic posing in front of every mirror. I'm speaking rather of the man God loves — the man created in God's own image, man the vessel of the Spirit of God, man the object of God's suffering love and redemption.

Jesus said, "What does it profit a man if he gains the whole world and loses his own soul?" If we cannot learn to love ourselves, accept ourselves, nurture ourselves in the relative weakness that is ours, the whole accumulated world gained by violence will do little good.

In our houses of worship we are to sit back and relax into the love and grace of God Almighty. After all, if God loves us, cares for us, even suffers for us, we have a significance and power no earthly kingdom can give. Let's do it now — relax, breathe in deeply, and say to ourselves, the Lord God Almighty of the universe loves me and affirms me as his own. The very hairs of my head are numbered. He knows me by name. I am esteemed and loved by God. I will, therefore, love and accept myself.

II.

But most men want to move beyond learning to love themselves; they want to be loved by others, especially women. How should women love men? *They should love physically and tenderly.*

This may sound strange coming from a pulpit. In the popular mind, physical, sexual love seems to be out of place in the church. Congregational churches especially are often associated with the New England Puritan tradition where it is assumed — wrongly — that sexuality and love were forbidden acts and subjects.

It was not the Puritans who were prudish about the matter of sex and sensuality; it was the Victorians. The Victorians — partly in reaction to the wild and bawdy Elizabethan Era — avoided speaking about sensuality and sexuality. For example, the famous Harvard psychologist William James had only two or three pages on sex in his two-volume work on psychology, and even then he admitted it was a distasteful subject to write about! How times change!

Nevertheless, the Victorians privatized the body and then the spirit. In their view men were more rational and women more earthly and sensual. But in the nineteenth century, women were elevated to a pedestal and regarded as more spiritual whereas men were regarded as less spiritual and less sensitive.

Strangely then, men began to be relegated to a lower, non-divine, somewhat animalistic, machine-like production unit. Perhaps this Victorian notion is best exemplified in what an elementary school girl wrote for her teacher: "Men are what women marry. They drink and swear, but they never go to church. They are more logical than women, but are afraid to feel something. Both men and women sprang from a monkey, but women sprang a little farther!"

Indeed, many women began to see men primarily as providers of home and security. It was their job to "bring home the bacon" and not only to "keep up with the Joneses" but to get ahead of them if possible. Consequently, men worked hard, still died seven years ahead of their spouses, transferring most of their wealth to them to enjoy as merry widows, if they could.

How can women love men? By helping them get in touch with their bodies again; by helping them feel more like a man than a production machine; by helping them get in touch with their sensory, sensual self; by helping them to be in touch with their feelings and emotions.

That is especially true if the great psychoanalyst C.J. Jung is correct that we men have a feminine dimension in us as well as the masculine. Jungian scholar Robert Johnson, in his book *He*, says women can help men get more in touch with their feminine role. How? By being themselves more feminine!

Professor James Nelson said recently to a group of ministers that "we have lost touch with the sensuous dimensions of the sacred." He went on to remind us that, after all, God expressed himself in body, in the sensuality of male and female, in the mysteries of masculinity and femininity.

But we men, so often ambitious, so driven, so over-scheduled and over-committed; we men, so preoccupied with getting ahead and with accomplishing just a little more before we relax; we men need help in getting in touch with our sensual, tender self again, and you women have unique powers to help us.

If the biblical Garden of Eden stories aren't enough to convince us, the sensuous Song of Solomon, this ancient Jewish wedding poem in our Bible, ought to help us along. After the man tells his maiden how pleasant and lovely she is, how her breath and kisses and breasts are beautiful beyond comparison, she says to him:

> *Come, my beloved,*
> *let us go forth into the fields,*
> *and lodge in the villages;*
> *let us go early and see whether*
> *the vines have budded,*
> *whether the grape blossoms*
> *have opened*
> *and the pomegranates are*
> *in bloom.*
> *There I will give you my love.*

She goes on to speak of mandrakes, which were thought to be an aphrodisiac, as well as the choice fruits and spiced wine she has for him. She then sighs,

> *O that his left hand were under*
> *my head,*
> *and that his right hand embraced*
> *me!*

All this in springtime when every man's fancy turns to love — how could we refuse! We can't, not if we are in our right minds. And you women can help us men become more physical and tender and loving with the powers of your love.

How should we love men? *We should love them with kindness and forgiveness.*

In the famous Pauline letter to the Ephesians, the writer advises Christians, "Be angry, but do not sin. Let no evil talk come out of your mouths, but only such as is edifying and fits the occasion." He advises us to put away bitterness, wrath, slander, clamor, and malice. And then in that famous verse we all should memorize, he says, "and be kind to one another, tenderhearted, forgiving one another, as God in Christ forgave you" (Ephesians 4:32).

In his *Newsday* story, writer David Behrens tells about a young couple who went to a pleasant brunch only to end up in an acrimonious argument over who was going to pay the check. He told of another couple where the date became upset because the man held the door for her. In another instance, the day after a pleasant date, a man sent over a box of chocolates only to receive a verbal bashing. And in another scenario, after dinner and a movie the couple went back to his apartment for dessert, but she fumed over why he put milk in her tea without asking and thus ended what had been a most pleasant evening.

Do we offend one another in our sexual relationships? Of course we do. Do we offend one another in our variety of relationships? Of course we do. Do most all of us have some cause for anger and revenge against those who have wronged us? If we were to take a poll to ask how many had been insulted, put down, cheated, hurt, lied to, treated unfairly or impolitely — how many would raise their hands? Most all of us have cause for a grievance of one kind or another.

That is especially true for women. While most of the violent crimes are men against men, many are indeed against women. In marriages, in crimes against the partner, ninety percent are committed by men, Lorena Bobbitt notwithstanding! If a woman is murdered or raped or beaten, police look first for lovers, husbands, estranged husbands, or other male acquaintances. We men have a terrible record when it comes to abuse of women.

Even so, women and others often can help the situation with patience and kindness and forgiveness. Of course, we do not mean that women should be doormats or remain victims in an abusive situation. Rather, they should get help and possibly get out.

However, Warren Farrell, author of several works to help men with self-identity, says he joined NOW — the National Organization for Women — in its beginning days, but he presently is critical of their work. Says Farrell, in the 1970's "the woman's movement was liberal, expansive, revolutionary, openminded. You might not agree with everything but you knew it was reaching for new truths."

But then he added it became somewhat analogous to Communism — becoming rigid and bureaucratic. Says Farrell, "Like almost all movements without opposition, it too has become totalitarian" (*Newsday*, 10-18-93, p. 44ff).

When any group or person becomes dogmatic or tyrannical or dictatorial or totalitarian, terrible injustices are bound to follow. While it is true that women have had and continue to have many grievances against men, it is also true that it takes two to tangle. Elton McNeil in his study of violence says, "Most homicides are preceded by angry quarrels in which the victim plays an active part in bringing about his own death" (quoted in May, *Power and Innocence*, p. 199).

Or to put it another way, if Helen of Troy had a face that launched a thousand ships, many a woman has a mouth that could launch a thousand fists! So have many men! A soft answer, as the Bible says, can turn away wrath. Be tenderhearted, not hard-hearted, says Paul. Forgive each other, give your life back to each other to start over again as God has given your life back to you.

How can we love men? We men need to learn to love and accept ourselves and to accept God's affirmation. You women can help us be more physical and tender. And we all need kindness and forgiveness. Doesn't this beat escalating the war between the sexes where nobody wins?

Prayer

Almighty God, creator and sustainer of the universe, whose energy has brought the universe into being and whose patient mercy sustains it from aeon to aeon and transformation to transformation, praise be to you for all the splendid wonders of the world we behold but never completely comprehend. You clothe your works in both majesty and mystery and shroud yourself with ineffable light. Yet it is in you that we live and move and have our being. We thank you for the gift of life.

You have been pleased to manifest yourself in our humanity, shaping us in your image, breathing into us your very breath of life. In primordial time you brought forth your first son of the earth, Adam, and imbued him with intelligence and freedom and the capacity to love and hate and create. In the terrifying experiment of human living you have made us something like yourself, able to create a future of our choosing.

We confess — especially we men confess — how badly we often have shaped history. In the midst of all our stellar achievements are the monuments of injustice, oppression, abuse, violence, bloodshed, war, and atrocities beyond description. The bodies of ravaged women and suffering children come vividly before our mind's eye. And we look out upon the world to see all the sorrow and crying, the wounds which will not be healed and the tears which never cease to flow. Almighty Father of us all, yours must be the largest heart of patience and mercy that ever could be. Forgive us, we pray, these terrible acts we perpetrate upon one another, especially us men who often have had responsible leadership roles.

But help us now, as Adams of the modern day, to think and create better, to develop and build more responsibly a peaceable life and world. If as men we have been churlish and callous, take away our fear and defensiveness and grant us courage to be thoughtful and caring. If we have been arrogant and greedy, release us from anxiety and apprehension so that we might be generous and gracious. If we have been egotistic and self-centered, draw us away from this self-suffocation to walk in the larger realities of your self-giving nature.

And if we have been discouraged and hurt and bruised, if we have been double-crossed and deceived and rejected, and if we have been victims of injustice and hate and even violence, raise us up and help us meet the new day with courage as new Adams for a new and better world.

In Christ's name we pray. Amen.

Discussion Questions

1. Male-bashing, according to some writers, has become popular today. Are American males the new "minority" to scoff at, ridicule, and put down? Are they the new scapegoats for society? If so, why? If not, why not? How do you feel about the issue?

2. Some observers say we have done a poor job raising boys and young men because so many of the fathers have been absent — absorbed in career, separated, divorced, or otherwise uninvolved in family. Consequently, boys have never learned how to be men from men, but have been taught how to be men by women. Do you agree? Disagree? Why? What steps might be taken to develop healthier boys and men?

3. Tenderness and forgiveness are sometimes regarded as unmanly traits. Do men of today feel that way? Are they out of touch with their feelings? If so, how can men find ways to be more expressive of emotions? How can women be helpful to them?

Chapter 5

How To Love Women

Above all these, put on love,
which binds everything together
in perfect harmony.
— Colossians 3:14

There it was, the cover article in the magazine *GQ, Gentlemen's Quarterly*, shouting at us in bold, black print: "Ah Women. What do they want from *us*? What do they fear? What makes them tick, makes them crazy, rocks their world — and why are they so _____ angry? Here in the paranoid, PC Nineties, loving women has never been dicier."

I think most men would agree. And if you think loving women has never been dicier, think how dicey it is for a man to stand up to speak on how to love women. In today's white-hot battle between the sexes, one hardly can utter an opinion without risk of verbal attack and assassination. Salvos are hurled back and forth from magazine to magazine, movie to movie, television sitcom to television sitcom, talk show to talk show, book to book, and in most every other form of media known to man (I mean humans)!

Saying a word on relationships between the sexes is a little like tiptoeing through the post-Gulf War mine fields of Saddam Hussein. The hidden mines of the war between the sexes are everywhere and just as treacherous and deadly as Saddam Hussein's hard metal type.

Comedian Milton Berle says, "When you don't praise a woman, she thinks you don't care anymore. Praise her and she thinks she's too good for you!"

Again he says, "If you want to know why they're called the opposite sex, just voice an opinion!"

If I could get by as a man talking about "How To Love Men," talking about "How To Love Women" is indeed chancy. One

53

woman suggested we ought to have a woman speak. She might be right. But should it be a lesbian, heterosexual, or bisexual? Should it be a mother, grandmother, or great-grandmother? Should it be a career woman, a mother and homemaker, or a combination of the two? Should it be Betty Friedan, Jane Fonda, or Sandra Day O'Connor, etc., etc.?

Amid the cacophony of voices (many of them strident), it is difficult to find a woman who fits as a spokesperson for all. Do you remember when Barbara Bush went to Wellesley College to speak at commencement as a wife and mother, only to have some Wellesley students question whether she was the kind of role model the college should be projecting for its graduates? Who should they have invited? Senator Kassebaum of Kansas? Jane Fonda? Connie Chung? Zoe Baird or Judge Kimba Wood? Or Julia Roberts? Or Barbara Walters? Oprah Winfrey or Roseanne Barr?

The endless variety of public women who have gained media attention points at the nature of the problem of loving women. Perhaps never before have there been so many different types of women, so many differing definitions as to what it means to be a woman, so many different female needs and demands expressed as in today's American culture. Is it any wonder then that not only men, but even women themselves, share considerable confusion over what it means to love and be loved?

Nevertheless, it doesn't take a genius to realize that what everyone seems to be craving is love. Listen to the songs on the radio. Aside from a few violent and sadistic songs and raps, they are mostly love songs. "What the world needs now is love, sweet love ..." we sing over and over again in a thousand ways, and that's what women need too — "love, sweet love."

How should we love women? I profess to be no expert. To be sure, I was raised by a loving mother (and father), and I had two younger sisters (as well as two older brothers). I now have a wife who is an associate minister. I have five daughters and one daughter-in-law, all college graduates. Our one son complained of all the females around in his growing-up years. But he and I did manage to have a male dog!

Does all that make me an expert on how to love women? Not on your life! They are more a mystery to me than ever. Nevertheless, the Christian faith has a lot to say about love — about true love and false. And some of the eternal verities of the Bible can be helpful in these high-pitched, humorless times in the war between the sexes.

Just how should women be loved?

I.

For one thing, women need to *be loved as a part of the Divine Reality.*

Judaism and Christianity have *not* been comfortable with thinking about the Divine Reality in feminine terms. It has been difficult for us to pray, "Our mother who art in heaven." Nearly all the terms for God in the Old and New Testaments are in the masculine gender. Almost all the allusions and references to God use male metaphors as opposed to female. Hymns, chants, liturgies, prayers, theologies and ethical systems nearly always have used the male noun or pronoun when alluding to God.

Consider the art of western civilization. The likelihood is that God will be depicted in male form. Take, for example, Michelangelo's famous painting of the creation of Adam found on the ceiling of the Sistine Chapel at the Vatican in Rome. God is portrayed unmistakenly as male rather than female. Observe other artistic portrayals of the deity and they are likely to be reminiscent of the popular old man with a long grey beard, sitting on a heavenly throne in magisterial elegance.

The idea of God as male is in many ways unique to Judaism and Christianity, and of course to Islam. The God of the Old Testament was understood to be transcendent, high and lifted up, beyond the reach of any human being, beyond the reach of earth itself. Earth could not possess him. The Psalmist sang, "I will lift up my eyes to the hills; from whence cometh my help? My help cometh from the Lord, *maker* of heaven and earth." Believing in a transcendent God, he saw God not *in* the hills, but *above* them. God was not the resident power or representative power *of* the hills, but the divine power *above* all the hills.

Likewise the high god of the desert of the ancient Israelites. Since they were on the move in the exodus from bondage in Egypt to liberation in the Promised Land, they believed they were following a *moving God*, a God who transcends ethnic identities and national boundaries. God was high and lifted up, surveying all the earth, not located in any specific place and therefore not bound by it.

Other religions and deities often were quite different. The most prevalent form of ancient religion was the fertility cult, in which there was not only a male god but also a female goddess. In Egypt it was Osiris and Isis. In Canaan it was Baal and Ashtarte. In the fertility cult, deity was projected in both genders — male and female.

While the prophets of Israel spoke out against the fertility cults and their idolatry and their sacred prostitution which exploited women, they did nevertheless affirm the feminine side of God. The feminine dimension of deity was affirmed in the very beginning, in the creation stories. "God created humankind in his own image; male and female created he them" (Genesis 1:27). In other words, femaleness, femininity, is as much an expression of the image of God as is maleness and masculinity. Both dimensions are necessary to complete the image of God in humanity, although the biblical God is above gender and cannot be contained by gender definitions.

Therefore, women do not need to deny their gender to be whole persons. The strong efforts of recent years to minimize sex differences and to promote unisex and androgynous notions of our human sexuality are fading, and rightly so. To be sure, gender roles of the past often have been means of oppression and exploitation.

But in the long run, women will do better to love themselves as women, as females, as feminine, as human expressions of the feminine dimension of the Divine Reality. And men will need to broaden their concept of Divinity to appreciate the feminine side, even though they often have thought of women as being "simply divine."

II.

How should women be loved? *They should be loved physically and tenderly.*

This kind of advice may seem either out of place in the church or irrelevant to the culture. As we have seen, the church has for many centuries suffered under the dualism and Manichaeism prevalent in its early years. One of the church's greatest thinkers and theologians, Saint Augustine, was, before his conversion, wild and libidinous in his sexual adventures. He then became a Manichaean, a dualist, wherein he disdained the body with its passions and desire. And when he became a Christian, he never quite gave up some of his Manichaen notions.

And three centuries before Augustine, Saint Paul seemed to downplay the importance of the physical in his writings. To be sure, he advised husbands and wives not to withhold themselves from each other except for periods of prayer and fasting. But in his early belief that the end of the age was at hand, he advised Christians not to marry, unless physical passion got the best of them. "It is better to marry than to burn," he told his followers, yet he preferred Christians would be like him — single and celibate — so they could serve the Lord.

The teachings of Paul and Augustine carried over into the Middle Ages in the development of religious orders and a single, celibate clergy. Marriage was okay for procreation, but celibacy was the higher way. Fulfillment of sexual passion was admissible to propagate the race, but spiritual passion to propagate the faith was indeed the higher calling.

That is why this lusty Song of Solomon from the Old Testament is such a helpful corrective. This ancient series of love poems, purportedly written by King Solomon in the tenth century B.C., but more probably written by an unknown author around 500 B.C., celebrates sensual, sexual love in high style. With the characteristic Hebrew emphasis on the importance and significance of the body, the songs radiate a rather intense sensuality.

Listen to some of the love language the lover has for his beloved:

> *Your cheeks are comely with*
> *ornaments,*
> *Your neck with strings of jewels.* (1:10)

As a lily among the brambles,
so is my love among maidens. (2:2)

He brought me to the banqueting
  house,
and his banner over me was love. (2:4)

You are all fair, my love;
There is no flaw in you. (4:7)

My beloved is all radiant and ruddy,
distinguished among ten thousand. (5:10)

How fair and pleasant you are,
O loved one, delectable maiden! (7:6)

Quaint lines to be sure, but you can bet no woman at the corporate water cooler has heard these before!

To be sure, we men are reluctant to say anything to women anymore. Since the Anita Hill testimony at the Clarence Thomas hearings, sexual harassment cases have doubled. Further, new and wide-sweeping legal definitions of sexual harassment have made men even more timid about saying anything to a woman, let alone attempting any flirtation.

But in the biblical view, the locker-room, knock-'em dead, wham, bam, thank you ma'am, macho man image was never appropriate. Read again the Song of Solomon and you have the image of something tender and sensitive and beautiful. The male lover depicted here is no brazen stud, "sperming" his way across America as many of our professional athletes and celebrities are doing.

No, what we have in the Song of Solomon is the ancient and beautiful divine dance between the sexes. It is the choreography of tender and respectful love, as remote from today's sensuous meat market mentality as the man in the moon. What is portrayed here is the tender, sensuous, respectful, almost reverential ballet of male and female, masculine and feminine.

To be sure, romance still lurks in the hearts of many Americans. The Harlequin romance novels are still read by millions. The romantic movie *Sleepless In Seattle* makes us believe there must be true love somewhere, even if our young son has to find it for us across the country. The novel and movie *The Bridges Of Madison County* has excited our sensuous and adulterous imaginations for a wild fling that eventually will fizzle in real life.

But the Bible would call us to respectful, reverential, non-exploitative physical, sensual, tender, committed love. The Bible teaches us that in loving women as women, loving them sensually and tenderly, we are loving God and ourselves. No cold, calculating, leering, libidinous exploitation is condoned by the Bible. Let us love as responsible, committed, sensual, tender persons.

III.

How should we love women? We *should love with patience and forgiveness.*

To be sure, men are as confused about women as women are confused about women. We have grown used to comments like these: "Whatever women do, they must do twice as well as men to be thought half as good. Luckily, this is not difficult." So said Charlotte Whitton, former mayor of Ottawa, Ontario. Novelist Erica Jong said, "Beware of the man who praises women's liberation; he is about to quit his job." The popular bumper sticker says, "After the Lord made man, he took a look and said, I can do better than that!" And Jill Ruckelshous said, "No one should have to dance backward all their lives," and some have added, "in high heels."

The rapidly changing roles associated with the women's revolution have made relationships confusing. As Lucy Kaylin, a woman writer, says in *GQ*, a men's magazine, men are "chauvinists if they pick up the check, losers if they don't, bullies if they take charge, hopeless weenies if they won't. They're being blamed for everything — like a couple of centuries of musty, white-guy domination — as countless mad-as-hell minorities chew up the scenery with their gripes" (February, 1994, p. 121).

She goes on to say that probably the relationships between the sexes have never been worse. "Call it the New Hostility, if you must — these days, the mood between men and women is growing far less libidinous than litigious, what with the once-collegial workplace becoming a hotbed of abuses and almost as many new categories of rape, suddenly, as Eskimo words for snow" (*ibid.*, p. 118).

The tension between men and women can be illustrated in the following dialogue. "You know, dear," the beleaguered husband said, trying to appease his wife, "I've been thinking over our argument and — well — I've decided to agree with you after all." She said, "That won't help you a bit — I've changed my mind."

In addition to that, the goals of the women's movement have changed. In the '60s and '70s, the young women who planned to be housewives plunged from two-thirds to less than a quarter — "an astounding shift in attitude in the flick of an apron. Child rearing became less a preoccupation than an improvisation, housework less an obsession than a chore" ("The Road To Equality," Nancy Gibbs, *Time*, Special Issue Fall1990, *Women: The Road Ahead*, p. 12). And this was the first generation to see almost half of all marriages end in divorce.

But today, young women seem to be affirming both family and career. They want a good marriage, two or three children, and they don't want their children in a child-care center or cared for by a stranger. Says Sheryl Hatch, twenty, a broadcasting major at the American University in Washington, "In the 1950s women were family oriented. In the '70s they were career oriented. In the '90s we want balance. I think I can do both" (*ibid.*, p. 13).

Perhaps she can, but it will take patience and forgiveness on the part of us all, especially men. In a time of rapid change, we are bound to experience severe emotional shock and dislocation. Most of us have been affected by the gender hostilities, the abrasive, prickly attacks, the peevish moods of anger and resentment, the disruption of life as we imagined and hoped it might be.

That's why these Christian virtues Paul speaks of are more important than ever. You will notice that he advises us not to take our standards from the prevailing cultural norms and moods. He asks us to put away from ourselves "anger, wrath, malice, slander, and foul talk." And he adds with profound insight, "do not lie to one another." Stop being deceitful. Take off these old character habits as you would take off dirty old clothes.

In their place, he advises us to clothe ourselves in a brand-new wardrobe which will go a long way to enhance our relationships. Put on these qualities like a new dress or suit. "Compassion, kindness, lowliness, meekness, and patience, forbearing one another ... forgiving one another ... And above all, put on love, which binds everything together in perfect harmony" (Colossians 3:8-14).

How do we love women? How do we love anyone? With these virtues, with these beautiful clothes for the soul from the divine character wardrobe. They will never go out of style.

Prayer

Almighty God, Creator of the universe and all the forms of life, out of whose being has come masculine and feminine, male and female, we praise you for the mysterious, magnetic powers within us which both attract and repel, and thank you that you have made us to participate in the divine dance of loving.

However, as athletes come to the coach and as musicians come to the master teacher, so we come to you, the master choreographer of all the human ballet, to acknowledge our missteps, our faulty sense of rhythm, our frequent inability to follow your divine impulses within. The dynamic interplay between us is often marred by a feeling of inferiority and defensiveness, by misunderstanding and resentments, by hostility and bitterness. O Divine Teacher of us all, forgive our willful inability to follow your lead and to celebrate fully the life to which you have called us.

We pray especially for the women of today. Made in your image and manifesting your divine nature, they so often have been maligned and misused. Containing within their beings the very powers of life, procreation, and nurture, they often have been oppressed, exploited, and abused. O God, enlighten all peoples of the world, especially men, that they might confess these wrongs and take action to amend their ways. Forgive us all, we pray, the wrongs we do to one another, and bring us to a better living.

We lift up our prayers to you for women with special needs. For women in oppressive economic, political, and social systems, we pray liberation and release. For women trapped in abusive marriages and relationships where their femininity is denigrated and their humanity scorned, we pray a way out to a fuller, more complete life. For women weary in well-doing, maintaining family values, and upholding spiritual principles, we pray an added measure of strength. For women overburdened with the cares of life and the concern of parents and children, we pray the refreshment of your Holy Spirit.

We pray especially for young women and girls. So many of them are so beautiful, so talented and capable, and yet so susceptible to destructive influences and corrosive companions. Help them, loving God, to resist all temptation, so that they might grow into their truest, most complete self.

And help us all in these trying days of strife and misunderstanding and violence, that we might come to the better way of life you have in mind for us.

Through Jesus Christ our Lord. Amen.

Discussion Questions

1. In the Bible God is usually depicted in the masculine gender. Does this make it difficult to think of the feminine as part of the Divine nature? Is it difficult to refer to the Deity in feminine terms? Would it help our love of women if we thought of the Deity as feminine as well as masculine?

2. Some Christians regard celibacy as a higher way of life than marriage. Is that an outmoded idea? Some people also regard chastity as old-fashioned and impossible to maintain. How should the Christian of today feel about these issues?

3. Even some women admit it is difficult for men to know how to love women today, since so many of the traditions, customs, and rules for relating have changed. Further, in the ongoing "war between the sexes," hostility seems to have increased. What advice would you have for men loving women in today's climate?

Chapter 6

The Subject Is Love

This is my commandment, that you love one another
as I have loved you. — John 15:12

We live in a love-obsessed world. Go to most any magazine
rack, and many of the cover stories have to do with love in one
way or another — how to attract a lover, how to stay in love, how
not to fall in love while enjoying sex, how to love again, how marriage and love can be compatible, and on and on.

Bookstores abound in how-to books on love, relationships, and
marriage. Romantic novels sell by the millions. Most all movies
have their requisite love scene as do most all novels, and by love
scene we mean the sex scene presented in some new and novel
way. The airwaves vibrate with love songs from tragic opera to
rhythmic rap or rock 'n' roll.

Yes, amid all the hate and violence, amid all the animosity and
mistrust, amid all the resentments and hatreds, amid all the broken
marriages and fractured relationships, most all would agree with
the old song that "what the world needs now is love, sweet love."
Most everyone would agree. Take a vote, and it would be nearly
unanimous: we all want and need love. On any given day in American society, in the bookstores, in the movies, on the talk shows, in
the music world, the subject is — yes, the subject is love.

But if the word "subject" is synonymous with "topic," the word
"subject" also has another meaning. In basic sentence structure,
we have a subject, a verb, and an object. The subject is the one that
somehow acts upon the object. For example: Dick hit the ball, or
Jane kissed Dick, or Dick ate the ice cream.

The curious thing is that in many ways we all want to be the
subject in the action. For example: John scored a touchdown, Henry
made one million dollars, Mary performed her one-hundredth

successful heart bypass surgery — each instances of the subject acting successfully upon an object to achieve a goal.

However, when it comes to love, many of us wish to retire into the passive role to be the object of love, the one to be acted upon to receive love. Many of the books and magazines are full of advice on how to make ourselves more attractive, alluring, and desirable so as to be the desired object of some ideal lover. We work to flatten the tummy, erase the wrinkles, build the biceps, improve the figure, enhance the wardrobe, and drive just the right car so we will be a desirable object of love.

Commendable as all this is and laudable though it might be, it rests on one large assumption, namely, that someone somewhere is going to be there to love us, that someone is going to be the subject in our sentence of perfect love, that some Tom, Dick, Mary, or Jane is going to embrace us as the object of lavish love. He or she will give, and we will receive.

As wonderful and romantic a scenario as that might be, our text draws us back to focus on the subject of the sentence of love, to concentrate on the one that is to be the actor in the love drama. If we all vote unanimously that what the world needs now is love, and if most all of us agree inwardly that what we personally need now is love, sweet love, our text asks us to think about being the subject of love, the actor rather than the acted upon, the one who is ready to give love as opposed to the one wanting to receive love. And our text teaches us several things about love.

I.

For one thing, the text teaches us that *love is an act of the will.*

That continues to surprise most people. Most people think love is an act of the emotions. We speak of love being blind and of falling in love and of love as someone seen across a crowded room on an enchanted evening whom you should never let go. Love, in many people's minds, is a matter of almost instant recognition and immediate affinity, like the young man standing up in a wedding, looking across at a bridesmaid he had never before seen and saying to his friend he was going to marry her. As it turned out, a year later he did in fact marry her.

Ah, romance. Thank God it still happens and sells millions of books and thousands of movies and makes our hearts flutter. Yet, when it comes right down to it, the Bible reminds us that in the last analysis, real love is an act of the will. Therefore, in our wedding ceremony, we shun the assenting words, "I do, I do," for the more affirming, assertive words, "I will, I will." "John, will you have Mary to be your wife, in all love and honor, in all duty and service, in all faith and tenderness...?" "I will," says John firmly and resolutely.

The idea that love is an act of will is found in Jesus' command to love one another, for as he says, this is my commandment, that you love one another as I have loved you. The notion that love can be commanded sounds as strange as the notion that morality can be legislated. "You can't legislate morals" is the popular saying. Yet what is such legislation if not the Ten Commandments and other moral principles put into civil law? We have laws against murder, stealing, false witness, rape, embezzlement, kidnapping, and on and on. If that is not an attempt at legislating morality, what is? Morality can be commanded because it is addressed to the moral will.

Likewise, love can be commanded by Jesus to his disciples because it is addressed not only to our emotions, but to our will, to the decision-making center of the self, to the inmost part of the self which determines self-identity. Love, in its deepest, richest, and most responsible dimension, is an act of the will.

Some of the Greek words for love are helpful in making the distinction between the kinds of love. For example, *epithemia*, sometimes translated love, means unbridled lust and greed, such as that demonstrated by a marauding army, pillaging, pilfering, and raping everything in its path.

Eros is familiar to us as erotic, as sensual, sexual love. But in its origins it means the upward, grasping, groping search for fulfillment — fulfillment which is sensual, emotional, intellectual and even spiritual. It is the "life force" in all living things, an innate drive and desire for fulfillment. It is a God-given drive, but by itself it tends to become greedy and self-centered.

Eros focuses on the object of love, seeking in the object the complete fulfillment of its longings and desires. *Eros* is more concerned to take love than to give it, to make the conquest than to be caught up in love.

Philia is the Greek word for "friend." A *philos* is a friend who reciprocates our love, a person who complements our personality, one who fulfills our wants and needs as we fulfill theirs. Friends mutually value each other, and hold each other in esteem, and take responsibility for loving each other. Their object is not so much to consume each other as to share and celebrate each other. So we often say of a husband and wife, it is ideal if they are not only great lovers but each other's best friend.

But in our text, Jesus uses that famous Greek word *agape* when he commands us to love as he has loved. *Agape* means to will the good of the other even when the other is unworthy or unlovely. It means deciding within oneself to be a loving person regardless of the beauty or lack thereof of the object of our love. Martin Luther King, Jr., had it right when he said that love in this sense does not necessarily mean liking but willing what is best, deciding to be a person of love, a subject willing to take the risks of loving even when the object of our love is somewhat repulsive.

In our text, Jesus is especially addressing his disciples, those that follow him, and therefore he is addressing us. At the very least he is addressing us in our marriages, in our families, and in our loving relationships. And he is saying to us, don't always wait to be the object of love. Instead, take the responsibility of being the subject of love, the one who is reaching out in risk and vulnerability to act in love rather than always waiting to be acted upon.

"Mary, will you have John as your husband, in all love and honor, in all duty and service, in all faith and tenderness...?" "I will." Love is an act of will.

II.

Our text also teaches us that *true love is an act of self-giving*.

Jesus commanded us to love as he loved, "greater love has no man than this, that a man lay down his life for his friends," which, of course, is exactly what we understand Jesus to have done for us.

Yet, self-giving is repugnant to many of us. We seek to find ourselves, to actualize ourselves, and to fulfill ourselves!

Aristotle urged self-realization and suggested persons are most moral when they seek to realize themselves. Humanist author Erich Fromm suggested our highest duty is to "take loving care of ourselves." And in its health-care advertisements, Mt. Sinai Hospital urges us to "take good care of ourselves" — and well we should.

Yet, Protestant scholar Lewis Smedes, in his excellent book *Love Within Limits*, warns of making the self a kind of idol. Then it is, says Smedes, that "we love others only so that they will be acolytes at the altar of our divinized self" (p. 55). Focused entirely upon the ideal self we want to become, we tend to become intolerant. We tend to reverse the sentence structure again, to force our partner to be the subject of love while we remain the object — passive and greedy.

But when love is understood to be an act of self-giving it motivates us to take responsibility to understand our partner in our relationship. And that takes some doing, says John Gray, author of the best-selling *Men Are From Mars, Women Are From Venus*. As a matter of fact, men and women are different — it is as if they were from two different planets.

In another of his books, titled *Men, Women And Relationships*, Dr. Gray says a self-giving man takes the responsibility of understanding the woman, and a self-giving woman takes the responsibility for understanding the man. As Jesus called his disciples friends, so should husbands and wives and partners be friendly enough to seek to understand the differences.

For example, in life and relationships, men tend to be focused and concentrated toward a goal, whereas women tend to be expansive and inclusive and concerned about relationships. Men tend to withdraw into an emotional "cave" to figure out things for themselves, whereas women tend to verbalize a variety of feelings in non-directive ways. Focused toward a goal, we real men, as the saying goes, don't ask for directions, whereas for women, asking for directions is a social occasion.

The approach of men and women toward life and relationships can be symbolized in wallets and purses, says Dr. Gray. A man characteristically carries a rather thin black or brown wallet with the bare essentials of driver's license, credit cards, membership cards, and paper money. A man is focused, efficient, intent on moving toward a goal with as few encumbrances as possible, including emotional ones.

But a woman sees life as a series of relationships, happenings and involvements. And her purse symbolizes it. Her purse characteristically is large and contains a wallet, coin purse, make-up kit, mirror, calendar, checkbook, calculator, hair brush, comb, three fingernail files, sunglasses, a package of tissues, several old used tissues, half-sticks of gum, keys and an extra set of keys, breath spray, dental floss, aspirin, vitamins, four or five pens (two of which work), a roll of film, lip balm, paper clips, rubber bands, matches, Bandaids, bobby pins, address book, picture album, and discount coupons, most of which are expired.

Shopping also points out differences. If men can shop for thirty minutes at most before becoming fatigued, many women see shopping as a way to expand their world and relationships. Women are expressive and expansive, more willing to talk out their feelings to discover who they are and what they feel. Therefore a wise man, problem-solver that he tends to be, will not rush in with a solution or minimize the problem. He will listen and listen patiently, realizing that women are different from men and that that is okay. He affirms her feelings and validates her concerns without minimizing them with a premature solution.

Likewise, women need to understand that men often make a statement after mulling it over for a period of time. Consequently, men tend to come off as authoritarian. But this does not mean the case is closed. Women should learn to ask questions about how he came to that conclusion and what factors have caused him to feel that way. Love as self-giving means thoughtful awareness of basic differences between men and women. It suggests a kindly friendship. Or as Dr. Gisele Kehl put it in her seminar, "A friend is glad to see you and doesn't have any immediate plans for your improvement."

III.

If love is an act of the will and an act of self-giving, it is also an *act of forgiveness*. Even on the cross Jesus said, "Forgive them, for they know not what they do." Forgiveness is at the center of God's loving, and he asks us to put it at the center of our loving.

In his great panegyric to love in 1 Corinthians 13, Paul said love is not resentful. It does not hold grudges. It forgives. It is willing to give the life back to start over again.

Dr. Lewis Smedes says, "Resentment is yesterday's irritation scratched into the sensitive membranes of our memory. It is yesterday's hurt grown up into today's indignation" (*op. cit.*, p. 74). And so partners tend to nourish old wrongs, harbor old hurts, and keep careful score of offenses so as to feel superior to the other. But, says Smedes, "Love lets the past die. It moves people to a new beginning *without* settling the past. Love prefers to tuck all those loose ends of past rights and wrongs in the bosom of forgiveness — and pushes us to a new start" (*ibid.*, pp. 78-79).

Once again, in relationships, many of us prefer to be the object of love rather than the subject. That way we can blame others for the wrongs in the relationship and continue to think of ourselves as the ones victimized. We adopt a martyr complex and place the blame on others, resenting them for their wrongs toward us. We deny responsibility.

As John Gray puts it, "Victims think they are not responsible for what happens to them or for how they feel ... Victims ignore their responsibility for provoking abuse in their relationships ... Victims are not willing to acknowledge how they contributed to their problem ... A sign of a victim attitude is the feeling of resentment and blame; there is a denial of responsibility." Therefore, "forgiveness is next to impossible when you cannot see how you are equally responsible" (*Men And Women And Relationships*, p. 31).

But the way out of a dysfunctional marriage, out of a dysfunctional relationship, is to give up the nourished resentments. We should let go of the harbored grudges, the carefully documented grievances on our emotional scorecard. Resentments manifest themselves in boredom, lack of passion, loneliness, and a sense of abandonment.

71

But if genuine forgiveness is experienced, the marriage can again be filled with passion and zest, and all the experiences of life once again fill up with meaning and vitality. We are to be tender-hearted, says Paul, forgiving one another as Christ forgave us, especially in our marriage and family (Ephesians 4:32).

There you have it — the subject is love. The subject is to be the lover, the self-giver, the forgiving one. As Christ's disciples, he commands us to love as he has loved. It isn't easy. But it is the secret of all life and the universe, because God is love. The subject is love, and we are the subjects.

Prayer

O Eternal God, Maker of the world and our Maker, who has caused all things to come to be and who sustains all reality by the power of your will, we praise and adore you and present ourselves before you in reverent worship. You call us forth from vanity and self-worship to acknowledge you as the source of all we are and can become. Grant us grace to hear your call.

In your presence, as in the presence of a master teacher, we become conscious of work not done, lessons not learned, knowledge not gained and insights not received. Catching a glimpse of your holiness and completeness we become aware of our potential we have not brought to completion and fulfillment. Looking into the realities of your patient, steadfast love, we feel contrition over our failure to love — especially those closest to us. In your mercy, be pleased to forgive us, O God.

If you have asked us to confess our sins, you have also urged us to ask you for assistance in our greatest needs. So we would pray for a renewed strength to love. See how frazzled our family life sometimes becomes, how stressed our marriages, how tension-filled our relationships, how fractured our friendships. There are times it seems harder and harder to get along, to live peaceably and harmoniously, to find joy and happiness in our living.

So, Dear Lord, be pleased to let your loving Spirit infuse us with strength to refresh us with the richness of true love. Grant us patience to listen and to understand. Enlarge our hearts with sympathy and compassion for the emotional needs of others. And help us to forgive others as you forgave us.

How earnestly we pray for the newly married, for the young families, for those seeking a life-mate, that all will be blessed by your wisdom and grace. For those long married, we pray refreshment, and for the widowed and lonely, we pray comfort and new fulfilling friendships.

Through Jesus Christ our Lord. Amen.

Discussion Questions

1. If love is regarded as an act of the will, are the romantic and spontaneous aspects of love thereby diminished? Does marriage understood as an agreement of two "wills" sound more like a business merger than the celebration of passion? What do you think?

2. In an age that encourages self-fulfillment and self-actualization and the development of self-esteem, how do we enable ourselves to be concerned about the partner's self-fulfillment, self-actualization, and self-esteem? Do we not then make ourselves objects and tools of the partner's selfishness?

3. Psychiatrist Karl Menninger in his book *Whatever Became of Sin?* says that in today's world everyone agrees that things are terribly wrong, but no one personally admits to doing anything wrong. Is it that way in love and marriage too — things are wrong but neither partner is willing to take responsibility for the wrong? If there is no confession of wrong, can there be forgiveness? Do partners actually forgive one another?

Chapter 7

The Object Is Love

In this is love, not that we loved God, but that he loved us and sent his Son to be the expiation for our sins. — 1 John 4:10

It was Victor Herbert who popularized a deep truth believed by many when he wrote:

Ah, sweet mystery of life at last I've found you.
Ah, I know at last the secret of it all,

For 'tis love and love alone the world is seeking.

'Tis the answer, 'tis the end of living,
For it is love alone that rules for aye.

And what again was that mystery? The mystery of life, as Victor Herbert and all lovers know, is love — yes, love at the heart of all of life's profound mysteries.

On our better days, most all of us would agree; although on other days, many of us would claim other realities as the mystery of life. Some would hold that power in its several forms holds the key to life. Others would claim fame and celebrity as keys to unlock access to all the soul's desires. Some would claim knowledge as the aim of all our living, whereas many others would exalt money as the ultimate key to life's mysteries, for money unlocks the door to most all of life's experiences, they would argue.

Nevertheless, Victor Herbert and all the romantics of the world wistfully believe it might be love for which we seek, love for which we long, love which we think might be the object of all our living.

In some quarters love might be criticized as sentimental feel-ings without much relation to reality. In other places, love is frowned upon as adolescent dreaming, or as the drive of millions of hormones firing in a newly sexually potent body. Others might trivialize love as the wish-dreams of the weak, or the rationalization of the losers in the high-powered competitions of life. And for cynics everywhere, love is, at best, a fantasy, a naive longing of the faint-of-heart for a world that never was and never will be.

Nevertheless, despite the cynicism, the negativism, and the rather roughshod repudiation of love as vital force, love remains the most talked about, thought about, sung about, dreamed about, and sought for reality in the world. Where would music, poetry, and literature be without love? What would happen to movies, theater, and publishing without love? Delusion or not, love is at the center of all our life concerns.

But there is a basic grammar to love. Previously we stressed the importance of being the subject of love in the sentence of love. If basic sentences have a subject, verb, and object, Christian love emphasizes first the importance of being the subject of love, the one who wills to love, the one who takes responsibility into himself or herself to act, to be the lover. Thus, in the sentence of love, "Dick loves Jane," Dick acts as subject to love Jane, the object.

But if every sentence needs an object, so does every lover. And the object of the object is to be loved, to receive love, and thus to complete love. Dick may be ready to love, but if Jane, for one reason or another, is unwilling to receive Dick's love, love is frustrated and incomplete. Just as the verb "to love" needs a subject, a love-giver, it also needs an object, a love-receiver.

As doctors Bonnie Maslin and Yehuda Nir say in their book *Not Quite Paradise*, love is not just an event. "It's an experience. It requires the mutual investment of two people in each other and in their partnership" (p. 1). Or to say it in another way, the sentence of love needs both subject and object participating in each other to make the verb "to love" complete.

So if previously we focused on the responsibilities of the subject in the love drama, we now focus on the responsibilities of the object in the love drama. For just as it takes certain requirements to be a lover, it also takes certain requirements to be the one loved. And this beautiful text on love from John's letter gives us some profound insights about the object of love.

I.

The first insight is this: *human love has its origin in divine love.* Or as John puts it in his famous phrase, "We love because God first loved us."

Various religions and philosophies have pictured God or the Divine in diverse ways. Some have seen the Divine as a changeless, disinterested, unmoved being without concern for human life. Others have more or less equated the sacred with the sexual life and fecundity. Philo, the brilliant Hellenistic Jewish philosopher, thought of God as pure mind. Moralists have thought of the Divine as pure righteousness and holiness. Those of a scientific bent tend to equate the Divine with energy, and others think of the Divine as the faceless, deterministic powers of Fate.

But it was the brilliant Aristotle, four centuries before Christ, who said God moves the world as the object of his love. Aristotle anticipated the Christian writers who came to see profoundly that God's primary gesture toward the world is not brute power nor callous indifference, but love. The Lord God Almighty expresses himself in love and seeks to love. Or, as John's gospel put it in the famous words memorized by every Christian, "God so loved the world that he gave his only begotten Son, so that whoever believes in him should not perish, but have eternal life" (John 3:16).

"In this is love," says John's first letter, "not that we loved God, but that he loved us and gave his Son as the expiation for our sins" (4:10). The Odes of Solomon put it this way, "I should not have known how to love the Lord, if he had not loved me. For who is able to distinguish love, except the one that is loved" (3:3-4).

So it is, Christianity makes the audacious claim that love is the ultimate reality, that love is the true essence of all things, that love — not brute power, not blind forces, not callous indifference, not deterministic fate — not these, but love is at the heart of all reality, because God is love. Not only that, but God, as the subject in the sentence of love, has acted toward us in love, even making himself vulnerable in love, risking himself in the suffering of his Son, to love us even when we were unlovely.

This idea is also central in Paul's thinking. We do not, says Paul, earn God's love by perfect observance of his laws. If God's love were dependent on our perfection, we would wait forever to receive it, since who of us can claim perfect law-keeping! By grace we are saved through faith. God, says Paul, acted toward us even when we were unlovely and hostile.

Therefore, human loving has its origins in Divine loving. We love, because God first loved us. Thus, all our loving in relationships, marriage, and family can be greatly enhanced if we receive the love of God into our lives.

II.

If John's letter teaches us that human love has its origins in Divine love, it also *teaches us to be responsible objects of love, recipients of love.*

That may sound like a strange teaching. Most all of us would say the real problem is teaching people to be the subjects of love, to be the one willing to take the responsibility to *do* the loving. Many of us would say the problem of loving lies precisely in everyone wanting to be the recipient of love rather than the giver of love. From the infant at the breast, to the demanding toddler of the terrible twos, to the self-conscious, self-centered adolescent, to the ambitious, goal-oriented, self-seeking, self-fulfilling career person, to the elderly person whose personal aches and pains are the world's only aches and pains in need of sympathy — in all these we want to be on the *receiving* end of love rather than the *giving* end. Even so, there are responsibilities involved in being good objects in the grammar of love.

For one thing, we have to be willing to acknowledge our need of love, our desire for love, our longing for love. One man told me he has no real joy in buying gifts for his wife because she never seems to need anything or want anything. When he does give her something special, she politely acknowledges it, forgets it, and moves on to other interests. As the subject in loving he has acted, but the object of his loving was not receptive in a loving manner.

A woman of my acquaintance said most of her overtures toward her husband went unheeded. He as much as told her he really didn't need her. He could get along quite well without her, thank you. As is typical, he became engrossed in his business and career. He identified emotionally more and more with the workplace than

78

with his wife and family and home. The love his wife and children tried to give him was short-circuited. He was wrapped up in himself.

Something similar can be said of some beautiful women. A strange paradox takes place in the heart of many men when they see a beautiful woman: they are at once powerfully attracted and then secondarily put off. The beautiful woman, on second thought, seems to be so perfect, so complete, so self-composed that she has no need for a lover. She appears to be in love with herself. She has admirers, worshipers even, but few if any real lovers, because they are afraid she is too arrogant really to need love or to receive it.

Thus, to be a good object of love we need to "be there" for our beloved. No matter how successful or knowledgeable, beautiful or powerful we might be, we need to humble ourselves before our beloved so as to be approachable, to be lovable. We need to break the shell of self-sufficiency to receive into ourselves the heart and soul of our beloved. As objects of love, we need to overcome selfish preoccupation with our own interests or career or problems or projects or priorities, to receive the overtures of love from our beloved acting as a subject toward us, his or her object.

If arrogance is a problem in the objects of love, so is its opposite, low self-esteem. One woman told me that she had experienced so much rejection in life, she found it difficult to believe her beloved really wanted to marry her. She had been beaten down so much, defeated so often, and pushed aside so frequently, she felt unworthy of love. She almost stopped believing in it. It was difficult to trust her beloved and to believe in herself.

Perhaps this is best illustrated in the musical, *Man Of La Mancha*, where Don Quixote meets the harlot Aldonza. "You will be my lady," he announces to the shocked prostitute. "Yes, you will be my lady, and I give you a new name — Dulcinea." And she laughs scornfully.

Don Quixote keeps affirming her, declaring her to be what he wants to believe she is. Later in the play, she is raped. She then appears on stage, hysterical, blouse torn, hair disheveled, dirt on her face, and terror in her eyes. And Don Quixote cries, "My lady!"

She screams back, "Don't call me your lady; I was born in a ditch by a mother who left me there naked and cold and too hungry to cry. I never blamed her. I'm sure she left hoping that I'd have the good sense to die."

Aldonza is weeping now, her head down, humiliated, wracked with shame. She then rises and screams, "Oh, don't call me a lady. I'm only a kitchen slut reeking with sweat. A strumpet men use and forget. Don't call me a lady; I'm only Aldonza. I am nothing at all." She then runs into the night, and Don Quixote calls after her, "But you are *my* lady, Dulcinea."

The curtain rises later to show the glorious dreamer of the impossible dream dying now, like Jesus, of a broken heart, scorned, laughed at, despised and rejected of men. Suddenly there comes to his side one who appears to be a Spanish queen in a mantilla and lace.

She kneels and prays. He opens his eyes and asks, "Who are you?" "Don't you remember? You called me your lady. You gave me a new name. My name is Dulcinea." She had received love and had become a new person. (Adapted from Robert Schuller, *Self-Esteem*, pp. 159-160.)

Many of us are either too self-denigrating or too self-important to be objects of love. We allow low self-esteem or arrogance to close us off to love. We wrap ourselves too much in the mantle of defensive lowliness or defensive self-righteousness to be truly open to love. We don't listen, don't heed, don't respond, don't take time, don't reciprocate, don't risk, don't make ourselves vulnerable, and won't take a chance on love. So the subject of love acting toward us in loving words and gestures cannot complete the sentence of love, because we are wrapped up in self-pity or self-importance. We have on the armor of fear and no one can pierce it.

But perfect love — that is, mature love — casts out fear, says our text. Fear separates; love unites. Fear utters reproach; love expresses acceptance. Fear is ready to defend with elaborate, legalistic self-justification; love is ready to confess its faults and needs. Perfect love, mature love, casts out fear — casts out fear in the object of love.

Or as theologian Daniel Day Williams put it so beautifully, "Love does not put everything at rest; it puts everything in motion. Love does not end all risk; it accepts every risk which is necessary for its work. Love does not resolve every conflict; it accepts conflict as the arena in which the work of love is to be done. Love does not neatly separate the good people from the bad, bestowing endless bliss on one, and endless torment on the other." Not that, says Dr. Williams. "Love seeks the reconciliation of every life so that it may share with all the others" (*The Spirit and the Forms of Love*, p. 138).

Yes, in the drama of loving, in the grammar of true love, there is a subject, verb, and object. Dick, the subject, who loves Jane has certain responsibilities as a lover. But Jane, as the object of love, has almost equal responsibilities — the responsibilities of openness, humility, willingness to share, the courage to take risks and to be vulnerable.

The English preacher-poet John Donne once wrote:

> *I am two fools I know,*
> *One for loving*
> *And for saying so*
> *In whining poetry.*

But we lovers know it is a divine foolishness. This loving, this risking, this vulnerability which accepts pain so as to affirm life's deepest pleasure. Ah yes, it is a divine foolishness. Victor Herbert was right:

> *Ah, sweet mystery of life, at last I've found you.*
> *For 'tis love and love alone the world is seeking.*
> *'Tis the answer, 'tis the end of living.*
> *For it is love alone that rules for aye.*

It is love that is the meaning of it all, for as John's letter puts it, the ultimate reality is love, for God is love. And we need to be open and receptive as objects of his love and that of our beloved.

Prayer

Almighty God, who out of the power of your Being has brought forth the universe, perhaps in the big bang, and who sustains it by the power of your word, seeding it with life here and there, nurturing it with minerals and water, praise be to you for giving us a self-conscious ride on spaceship earth. We have come from you — from the dust of the earth which you made, and from your vital Spirit, breathed into us to make these dust-composed bones to walk around. We praise you and give you thanks.

However, you have brought us into a world where pain competes with pleasure. You have given us an existence where the sublime is clouded with suffering, and where the agonies of life seem at times to outweigh the ecstasies. In fact, it seems as those who love most suffer most, and those with compassion seem most readily hurt.

Therefore, in your divine presence we lift our prayers for those who suffer. We think of many within our circle doing battle with cancer in its many forms. We call to mind the debilitating illnesses for which there seems to be no cure. Our hearts go out to those maimed in body, and we lament those troubled and distressed in soul and mind. Even now in our hearts we name those in need of your healing and the revitalization of your Spirit.

We also call to mind peoples of the world who suffer from oppression and exploitation, for the huddled masses of poor yearning to breathe free. Reawaken in us all the dream of Martin Luther King, Jr., where the subjugated, the poverty-stricken, the disadvantaged, the dispossessed, the down-and-out, the discriminated against — where all might come to a better day of sharing the world's fabulous wealth and have a more equal opportunity to grow and to develop to their best potential. Help us to be dedicated to that dream.

And now by your grace, infuse us with a new resolve to be open to love, to see again the overwhelming mysteries of your living world, to appreciate anew the glory of the human body and mind and soul, and to celebrate your gift of love which you are waiting to give to all receptive souls.

Through Jesus Christ our Lord. Amen.

Discussion Questions

1. In an era critical of "co-dependency," could it be said that love and marriage are in some ways an unhealthy co-dependency? In a time when both men and women are encouraged to be independent and self-sufficient, does not the idea of making oneself vulnerable as the lover or as the loved destroy self-sufficiency and independence?

2. Some people feel unworthy of the partner's love, especially if the partner is "above" them in education or socio-economic status. Is it a dangerous thing to marry outside of one's "social class"? Will one partner always feel superior and the other inferior?

3. Some lovers seem blind to the faults of their beloved, as Don Quixote seemed blind to who Aldonza really was. Other lovers see the faults of the partner and feel they will be able to change and improve the partner to make them into the kinds of persons they want them to be. What is your opinion on these ideas? Is there a "perfect partner" for everyone?

Chapter 8

Hungers Of The Heart

There is no fear in love, but perfect
love casts out fear. For fear has to
do with punishment, and he who fears
is not perfected in love. We love,
because he first loved us.

— 1 John 4: 18-19

A while ago a college girl asked me a very profound question. "Why," she asked, "did God ever create us in the first place? What is the purpose behind it all?" It was one of those questions where you take a long, deep drink of your coffee before you answer. Or, if you are a pipe smoker, you do what pipe smokers always do: you take your time relighting your pipe while your mind races for an adequate reply.

I delayed as long as I could while I searched for an appropriate response to that ancient and perplexing question. Whatever other reasons there may be for God's creating us, the basic reason must have to do with love, I said. From the Christian point of view, God created us because of love.

Sincere and intelligent, I could almost see her mind working as she formulated the next observation. "It surely must have been risky, " she replied, "and I'm not so sure he is succeeding or that love is winning out in our kind of world."

I told her that I agreed with her, and that on my "down" days I also wondered if the world wasn't just some universal accident where chance and brute power win out over tenderness, thoughtfulness, and compassion. But on the good days, when all is going well, when God is in his heaven and all is right with the world, I have a renewed commitment to the reality of love.

But, of course, my commitment to the reality of love in a world like ours is based on more than subjective feelings and whether or not I need sleep or have indigestion. My commitment to the reality

85

of love is based on the Christian conviction that God has revealed himself in love by acting in creation and re-creation.

The writings of "John" assert over and over again that God is love, as does the whole New Testament. And this love, as we know it, does not exist in isolation. Love is relational. It is known in relationship. More than that, love, to be real, must be free. Forced love or computer-programmed love is no love at all.

Love is free, radically free, and therefore radically risky. Consequently, many of us are anxious and fearful about the risks of loving. Yet John's letter asserts that "perfect" or mature love overcomes the fear. God has made us in his image to be free, to think, to choose, and therefore to love. And like God, we do not want to live in isolation. Love, by its very nature, must take the risk to give love as well as the risk to receive love. And we are vulnerable in both the giving and the receiving. Another college girl said she felt those who love the most stand the greatest chance for getting hurt. I think she's right.

Nevertheless, it is by our very nature that we hunger and thirst for love. We long for that which can fill us up, make us complete and whole. As the body craves that which will give it sustenance and health, so the heart craves that which will give it affirmation and significance. We long for love, we crave love, some of us desperately, even pathetically, as we search for love wherever it can be found.

The hungers of the heart can be summed up in one word — love. But love has several dimensions for which we crave. And they include compatibility, passion, and communication.

I.

Let us consider *compatibility*.

Will Rogers used to say that the way to succeed in the stock market was to buy a stock low, and sell it when it goes up. "But what if it doesn't go up?" someone asked. "Then don't buy it," said Rogers.

We might paraphrase Rogers to say that the way to succeed in marriage is to marry someone with whom you are compatible. "But what if you marry and find that you are incompatible?" someone asks. "Then don't get married" would be his too-late, never-win advice.

Compatibility has to do with personality types, habits, manners, education and social class, life-goals and lifestyles, backgrounds either adequate or inadequate, religion and value systems. Maurice Chevalier once quipped that many men fall in love in light too dim to choose a good suit! By themselves, emotion or chemistry may not be good judges of compatibility.

Therefore, people contemplating marriage should look seriously at the habits, manners, values, customs, and goals of the proposed partner. Do you want and expect similar things in life? Children, for example? One couple coming for pre-marriage counseling had a serious difference. She wanted children, he didn't. She married him anyway thinking she could change his mind. She couldn't and now they are divorced.

Do you want dinner in the dining room or around the television? Do you want your children to go to public schools or private? In what religion will you raise your children? Do you like to take similar vacations? And do you have similar priorities on how you spend or invest your money? How about taste in clothing, house, and furniture? What about families, hobbies, and special interests?

While none of us wants to marry a clone, why should we want to marry someone who approaches life from an opposite point of view? Each of us has a right to be who we want to be, and to want what we want, but then we may not be right for each other. Is it not wiser to recognize that from the beginning? We all want to buy the "stock that will go up"! But if you are incompatible in courtship you likely will be incompatible in marriage. Why not recognize that and break it off before it's too late? Better the pain now than later.

And how about people planning their second or third marriage? Some people are even on their eighth or ninth marriage. Joey Adams likes to pick on Elizabeth Taylor, referring to her as Elizabeth Taylor Hilton Wilding Todd Fisher Burton Burton Warner. And Cary Grant said that Elizabeth Taylor is writing a new book about her boyfriends — she's now up to chapter 46. And Sinatra adds that she no longer gets a new marriage license. She just pencils in the name of her latest husband.

But most of us are not on our ninth or tenth marriage. However, some of us may be approaching a second or third marriage. Most divorced people do remarry as do many widows and widowers. Do not many of the same principles hold true? We have deeper hungers of the heart for companionship and compatibility, and many are "older and wiser" the second time around, but many are not. Witness the even higher divorce rate for second and third marriages.

Everybody knows about "marrying on the rebound," but many people do it anyway, thinking it will be different for them. But often it isn't. When we are single we can get so lonely, so down, feeling hurt and anger and guilt and rejection. Widowed or divorced, our sexual passion may even increase during singlehood and we seek erotic companionship as well as friendship.

Nevertheless, our judgment is sometimes not balanced for a while after divorce or death of a spouse. Determined not to marry someone with the faults of our former spouse, we overcompensate and marry someone who doesn't have the faults but may not have the virtues either.

That is why family and friends are so important. We need a close circuit of associates. If we feel reluctant to introduce our new friend to family and friends, chances are we will have a reluctant marriage. If the new friend balks at our lifestyle and is uncomfortable with our deepest values and is unsure about our children, chances are the discomfort will increase.

True in our singleness, we may think we are running out of time. A friend of mine had a great-grandmother who outlived three husbands, and at age 93 was about to marry a fourth. Since she had known the man only two months, her family discreetly suggested she might give the courtship a little more time. "Listen," she replied, "at my age I don't have much time!"

Perhaps at any age we may feel we don't have much time to satisfy these deep hungers of the heart for compatibility. But whatever the time, genuine compatibility is one of the deep satisfactions of love.

II.

Another hunger of the heart is that of *passion* — deep feeling and emotion.

It has to be confessed that Christians have been somewhat afraid of passion. Emphasizing commitment, fidelity, and stability in relationships, the church has been identified often thereby with stultifying, middle-class boredom. Concerned to hold together the fabric of family and society, Christianity has sometimes erred on the side of plodding duty and conventional profitability over genuine feeling and passion.

In his book *Love in the Western World*, Denis de Rougemont has suggested that our urbanized, technocratic culture often denigrates passion in favor of regularity and predictability, no matter how boring. We often reduce ourselves to an updated feudal system, making ourselves mere economic production units or serfs in the giant money-making machine. Passion is easily repressed and sublimated for the sake of production.

Christianity's fear of passion has something to do with the ancient world in which it arose. In that world, passion was often the ruling force. Fertility cults abounded everywhere. In Ephesus, one of the important early centers of Christianity, there was a huge temple to Artemis, the fertility goddess. Sacred prostitutes and phallic symbols abounded with many of these cults. Sexual looseness and promiscuity were common and marital fidelity was perhaps the exception more than the rule.

Another factor was the doctrine of dualism where it was believed that the body and its desires were degrading and unspiritual. Through St. Augustine and others, dualism helped produce monasticism and the doctrine of celibacy. Christians, and later the Victorians, were somewhat embarrassed by the body and its desires and drives.

However, it is precisely this dualism which John's first letter attacks. The High God of Mind and Spirit is not remote from the material world of flesh and desire, says John. On the contrary, it is this very world which is the self-expression of the creative love of God, and it is precisely this world of flesh and desire that Jesus entered to redeem.

Therefore, Christians should not regard sexual passion as bestial (as one woman told me), or inhuman (as some Christians have thought), or as a necessary evil you go ahead and do if you feel you have to (as one woman told her husband). Christians should not, like Victorian psychologist William James, regard it as a bit distasteful to discuss, devoting as he did only a page or two to the subject. Sexuality, maleness and femaleness, passion and desire, are a part of the expression of the very image of God. God created us male and female and called it good.

Therefore, we Christians should take the lead in creative and positive teaching to ourselves and our children on this crucial subject. And if we feel sexual passion controls the world today, and if we see the powers of eros abused and exploited by Hollywood and advertisers, we must affirm, nevertheless, that God ordained these powers and intended we use them not only for procreation, but for the satisfaction of the deep hungers of the heart.

In many ways the younger generation has been correct in its critique of the older generation. The older generation sometimes gets caught up in obligation without joy, economic commitment without freedom, social consciousness without private play.

If the young are too "now oriented," lacking planning, the older are too "future oriented," lacking spontaneity. If the young need to "buckle down," the older need to "lighten up." If the young need to take social obligation more seriously, the older need to be released from past hang-ups, worrying too much about what people will say.

Older couples often have commitment but not passion. Friendship may be there, but little feeling. Too often they have let routine degenerate into boredom. Familiarity has bred a mild contempt. For the sake of duty they have negated spontaneity and playfulness.

The young are right. We need to relight the fires of passion within our marriages. We need to relax, to rediscover the body with its mysteries and wonders. We need to change the routine, to lighten up the schedule, to celebrate our God-given maleness and femaleness, which in ecstatic union is an expression of the divine love — perhaps one of the few places we experience the divine.

III.

In addition to compatibility and passion, our hearts have a deep hunger for genuine *communication*.

Many couples have fallen into bad habits when it comes to communicating. A *New Yorker* cartoon shows a man buried behind a newspaper while his wife explains to her woman friend, "He knows what I'm going to say, and I know what he's going to say, so we never talk!" Indeed some of the excitement implicit in an affair is uncertainty of what the other person will say or do. Conversely, boredom sets in when we take the other for granted or when we shut the other out.

Norman Cousins once lamented the lost art of conversation in modern society. "Modern conversation," says Cousins, "is waiting for the other person to stop talking so we can talk. Everyone is talking. No one is listening."

Many couples have lost the companionship of good communication because they no longer really listen. Consequently, we need to bite our tongues, open ourselves to our mate, and receive the feelings and insights that person longs to share. We need to ask questions to draw the other out. We need to seek out how the other feels without being so quick to let him or her know how *we* feel.

Our hunger for communication may best be expressed in poetry.

> *I've been wanting to tell you who I am*
> *to sit down in a long talk*
> *with a warm room around*
> *with solid walls and no voices*
> *outside or screams or screeches*
> *to interrupt the speeches I've rehearsed*
> *long hours in silent thoughts upon my bed.*
>
> *I've been wanting to tell you who I am*
> *maybe on a long trip or vacation beach*
> *with the rhythm of ocean wind and surf to beat*
> *courage into my bones and assurance*
> *into my heart that it's worthwhile,*
> *that your knowing smile would not be*
> *a facade for condescending indulgence.*

91

I've been wanting to tell you who I am
maybe after the children are asleep
and the guests have all gone home
leaving an afterglow of human warmth
in which we might bathe our cold hearts
and massage them to responsive life again
to receive the knowledge of who I am.

I've been wanting to tell you who I am
and yet, I thought it probably could wait
'til after the bills are paid and the checkbook balanced
— as if we ever could — balance the checkbook I mean
— and not our lives of course — who could balance
them since I'm afraid to tell you who I am?

I've been wanting to tell you who I am
My God — I've been wanting to take you into
inner space aboard my spirit
— searching as it is for a kindred
spirit of openness and quest and not the
static, placid rest of death
under the wistful gaze of memory's regret.

I've been wanting to tell you who I am
to say it right out in the open except
I'm not sure what to say and can talk only
in images and symbols and things that balk
at concise formulation and precise calculation
since my spirit doesn't soar that way,
and whoever I am, I'm not in a box.

I've been wanting to tell you who I am
to get you aside from preconceived notions
of who you think I am or ought to be
which is also me, unrealized, of course,
buried, dormant and in reserve,
or bewildered in a maze of non-expectancy.

I've been wanting to tell you who I am
but I've been afraid you'd think
my dreams adolescent dreams and
my thoughts immature thoughts and

myself a dependent self in need of
an independent self, like yourself
a father-mother image of a perpetual child.

I've been wanting to tell you who I am
to clean out the anger, to let the
hostile fires flame out in purging fury
the dross of our relationship and the
accumulated crud of protective indifference
which hang around my spirit's neck like
an albatross — grounding my potentiality.

I've been wanting to tell you who I am
but it's quite a lot and if I got
started I'm not sure I'd get stopped
except maybe by your not-too-well covered yawn
or your next meeting or appointment,
not that I don't have some of my own,
so why begin what never could be ended?

I've been wanting to tell you who I am
and it's not pleasant, neither the telling nor the hearing,
so I'm leering to this side and that in avoidance
of your calm, cool countenance of disdaining
contempt of my shaky fears and non-coherence
of my depths no longer concealed,
now revealed to your careful confidence.

Yes, I've been wanting to tell you who I am
by the fire on a rainy Sunday afternoon maybe
or overlooking the gentle valley from a soft autumn
hill, or anywhere or time I thought you would listen
or accept my remorse and my regret for things
that might have been or ways I might have loved
but haven't yet, because I'm afraid to tell you who I
am and unsure you'd like what I might become.

"I've Been Wanting To Tell You Who I Am"
by Maurice A. Fetty

Prayer

Eternal God, who out of the mystery of your Being decided to create the world male and female, and who out of your wisdom has placed within us the powerful forces of attraction and repulsion, we thank you for making us a part of your self-expression and praise you for making possible our experience of the ecstasies of love. You have conceived the world in love and have intended for each of us to be begotten in love, nurtured in love, and to find in love our eternal destiny. We thank you for these promises.

When we are honest we must confess love often to be absent from our own hearts and minds. Many of us have become preoccupied with our own concerns. We want to be heard, but we rarely listen. We want our dreams to be realized with little regard for dreams of others. We want sympathy for our feelings while granting little sympathy for the feelings of others. In short, we confess we want to be loved without taking responsibility for the loving. Forgive our smallness and selfishness, O Lord, and grant that we might have strength and courage to be responsible lovers.

We pray especially for husbands and wives that their love might be refreshed and renewed. For those whose love is locked in stalemated arguments, we pray new insight and change. For those marriages where one partner does all the giving, the other all the taking, we pray new self-esteem and confidence so that both might equally give and receive. For those couples gripped by anger and overborne by grudges of years passed, we pray the strength to forgive and the openness to begin anew. For husbands and wives who have let passion turn cold and intimacy evaporate, we pray a renewal of the fires of desire which you intend for them. And for those whose love is healthy and robust, grant that it may grow from strength to strength.

And for those who are single we pray; and those newly separated or divorced, that they might have strength to cope and not be seduced by false, exploitative love; for those widowed, that love of friends and your divine love might give them strength and healing; for those unable to find that very special one to love, that in your providence they might come to fulfillment; for young people coming into the full and sometimes terrifying powers of desire, that they might know how to control love and remain chaste; for all the lonely and forgotten and forsaken, that new friendships might be formed, so that a measure of the hungers of our hearts might be filled.

In Christ's name we pray. Amen.

Discussion Questions

1. Many believe that "love conquers all" and that questions about compatibility take the romance out of marriage and reduce it to more of a business partnership. How do you feel? Should couples discuss their compatibility in such areas as careers, money, children, communication, sex, and religion? How might couples balance concerns about romance and compatibility?

2. If some couples emphasize romance, others emphasize practicality. Are couples today too involved with careers, children, and bills to have time and energy for passion? If passion is waning, what might couples do to light the fire of romance again?

3. Communication is a lost art in many relationships, so much so that many people feel lonely and abandoned, unable to share on a deeper level with a "soulmate." If communication has broken down between partners, what steps might be taken to repair it and improve it? If boredom has set in, how might couples enhance the relationship?

Chapter 9

Intimate Partners

And above all these put on love,
which binds everything together
in perfect harmony.
— Colossians 3:14

The Beatles have surely made an impact on our culture. I heard the other day that their song, "Yesterday," has been played millions of times in recent years. "Yesterday, all my troubles seemed so far away ... Oh, I believe in yesterday."

Another of their songs made famous was "Eleanor Rigby." It is a song about a woman in bridal dress and veil waiting at the church with Father McKenzie, only to discover she had been abandoned by her beloved. "All the lonely people, Where do they all come from?"

They came from abandonment and forgottenness.

If we could get people to talk about feelings and longings of their inmost heart, no doubt many would speak of a sometimes deep and pervasive loneliness. For many, it is perhaps the deep, inward dread of death, the terrible gripping realization of our mortality that comes in upon us with intense and silent power.

It is that innate understanding underlying all our getting and achieving, underneath all our acquisitions and successes, that some day we face an unknown annihilation, a passing away from present consciousness and awareness where we lose control totally. It is the terrible dread of this immense unknown, this lonely valley we all, like Jesus, have to walk alone.

Is it any wonder then that we seek companionship in what is sometimes so terrifying a life? If in being thrust out of the womb we come into a sometimes cold, harsh, and always uncertain world, is it any surprise we seek connectedness and relatedness, a strong sense that we are not alone, a sense that someone is there with us, feeling and seeing and understanding as we do? In short, in the face of this world's loneliness, we long for intimacy.

Francine Klagsbrun, in her book, *Married People*, suggests that "of all the components of marriage, intimacy is probably the quality most longed for, and often the most elusive." Klagsbrun continues, "Sexual intimacy is major, of course, but intimacy in terms of closeness and affection between partners goes beyond the sexual aspects of marriage. With that closeness many things become possible. Without it, inside as well as outside marriage, there is loneliness" (p. 18).

Indeed there is. One of the pervasive emotions is that of loneliness. Americans huddle together in huge metropolitan regions for many reasons, but one of the major reasons is to stave off loneliness. If our pioneer ancestors braved the wilderness alone and staked out an isolated homestead on the lone prairie, their descendants take their chances on the noise, congestion, and frustration of the city in order to be with people.

I remember living in New York City during the Cuban missile crisis. Every time we heard strange noises overhead, we New Yorkers looked up expecting to see a Russian missile zeroing in. Rather than moving to the big sky, lonely reaches of Wyoming, out of the reach of Russian missiles, New Yorkers resigned themselves to their common fate of being together.

Perhaps some marriages have a similar mentality — that of staying together no matter how much the frustration and aggravation. It beats the loneliness they might have to endure if they called it quits.

The large number of divorces indicates that America is still the land of the free. Sure, but the increasing marriage rate shows that it's still the home of the brave. And remarriage is, as the saying goes, the triumph of hope over experience.

Nevertheless, our hope of achieving an intimate partnership is more than just maintaining a stalemate for the sake of companionship. Our goal is more than a desperate struggle against the dread. Rather, we look for that unique magic between a husband and wife that is more than chemistry, more than fate — a magic that comes about in the mystery and miracle of human loving. We look for an intimacy which arises out of Paul's advice: "And above all these put on love, which binds everything together in harmony" (Colossians 3:14).

I.

As much as we long for intimacy, we have difficulty balancing it with the longing for *freedom* and *self-fulfillment*.

Some years ago, psychologist Erik Eriksen described intimacy as "the capacity to commit himself to concrete affiliations and partnerships and to develop the ethical strength to abide by such commitments even though they may call for significant sacrifices and compromises" (Quoted in Klagsbrun, *op. cit.*, p. 19).

It is precisely those sacrifices and compromises we are not sure we want to make. Just what is the price of intimacy? Does it mean giving up true self-fulfillment? Many advice books of recent years have criticized notions of self-sacrifice and self-giving as being harmful and detrimental to the self. Many married people have been lured out of marriage with the goal of finding and realizing true self. For them marriage was oppressive, burdensome, and stifling. Many marriage partners (more women than men) have seen themselves as adjuncts or accessories to the partner's ego and career and consequently have never attained a kind of self-fulfillment on their own terms.

In his book, *Habits of The Heart*, Robert Bellah notes, "The sharing of a commitment in a love relationship can be seen for some to swallow up the individual, making her (more often than him) lose sight of her interests, opinions and desires" (p. 93). If one partner becomes a kind of doormat or nonentity she or he can become exploited, manipulated, dominated, and ignored. It is no wonder that in today's freer climate many people get out of that kind of relationship.

Nevertheless, unless one lives as a hermit, relationship with anyone requires some giving of the self, some losing of the self, in order to gain a dimension of some other self. After all, most of us readily give a large portion of the self to business or profession or career. Consider the discipline needed to be a professional athlete or musician, or the dedication and training needed for some of the professions. We give of ourselves, sometimes too much of ourselves, to be a success in career. Therefore, is it not reasonable to expect that we shall have to give of ourselves in marriage to achieve a greater intimacy?

Shyness and insensitivity may be a problem for some. George was so shy, but he finally asked Judy for a date and they went horseback riding. When they stopped, the two horses began nuzzling each other affectionately and George said wistfully, "Now that's what I'd like to do." And Judy said, "Go ahead — it's your horse!"

The interplay of individuality and intimacy are symbolized in what couples do with the unity candle during their wedding ceremony. In the "old days" couples would use the two outside candles to light the center one, symbolizing their union, and then would blow out the side ones symbolizing their individuality as swallowed up in the new union. But not so today. Many couples want to leave the side candles burning to symbolize that they still are individuals with individuality despite the oneness of their marriage.

Of course, the biggest change has been brought about by the women's revolution. In the nineteenth century, de Tocqueville observed that the woman's role was confined to home and family. If money and hard reason ruled the world, in the home the wife and mother ruled with love and compassion. Put on a pedestal, and then, as Joan Rivers says, expected to dust it, women were to pass on the mores and restrain the men. The devotion and unselfish love of women were seen as the most visible example of morality.

If on the American frontier or in the urban ethnic neighborhood, economic necessity and mere survival bound a husband and wife together, today economic freedom often means freedom from marital commitments. If a measure of intimacy was once forced upon us by necessity and tradition, we now are more free to pursue intimacy wherever we may find it.

Thus, in our economic and social freedom, we are free to pursue our psychological gratifications aside from traditional roles. Therefore, says Robert Bellah, "The love that must hold us together is rooted in the vicissitudes of our subjectivity" (*ibid.*, p. 90). More than that, says Bellah, "finding oneself is not something one does alone" (*ibid.*, p. 85). We know ourselves and find ourselves in relation to other people. But when we step outside normal traditions and roles, intimacy may be a little more difficult, a little more elusive.

On the other hand, we can be freed up to share our true selves with one another. Consequently, we ironically must enter into marriage with more commitment, not less, more responsibility than less, because traditional norms and roles are not assured. Subjectivity becomes more important than objectivity.

The irony is that in order to find the self we must in a sense lose the self to our beloved. We give and then are better prepared to receive. While the great commandment enjoins us to love our neighbor as ourself (and our spouse counts at least as our neighbor), the great commandment does assume we shall have a healthy love of self. The world's great commandment, "look out for number one, period," assumes a love for the self but ignores God and the neighbor and the spouse, and thus enters into a life of true loneliness.

All the lonely people, where do they all come from? From people who love only self and are unwilling to risk the self in the love, in the adventure, of intimacy.

II.

If intimacy requires the risk of giving the self as well as fulfilling the self, it also implies *acceptance* and *trust*.

In his many interviews with married couples, Robert Bellah and his associates talked with Nan Pfautz, a divorced secretary in her mid-forties. After being single for a considerable time, she fell in love and remarried. Why would she do that after an unhappy first marriage? It had to do with a developing sense of intimacy which overcame the terrible loneliness.

She told the story this way: "I let all my barriers down. I really was able to be myself with him — very, very comfortable. I could be as gross as I wanted, as silly as I wanted. I didn't worry about or have to worry ... about what his reaction was going to be. I was just me. I was free to be me" (*ibid.*, p. 91).

Many couples for whom intimacy is real speak in a similar way. One couple interviewed said that intimacy and acceptance means knowing that at bottom we all have a "creepiness" about us, and that we are accepted anyway. Most couples know "secrets" about one another and their family but affirm each other in spite of that.

To be sure, there may be the danger of sharing too much, of baring the soul too extensively, of saying things better left unsaid. Yet the ability to share deeply, to confess each other's weaknesses and not be put down or destroyed or to share dreams and ideals and not be laughed at, are important functions for the development of intimacy. Many of us treasure the security of knowing that someone knows us, warts and all, and accepts us and loves us nevertheless. Despite Groucho Marx's delightful insight into snobbery where he quipped he wouldn't want to join a club that would have him as a member, most of us would welcome being joined to a partner who accepted us fully with all our foibles.

III.

But if acceptance and trust are important for intimacy, so are *vulnerability* and *exclusiveness*.

Loving is always risky for it means opening ourselves up to the other person both physically and emotionally. (By the way, despite the contemporary practice of rather indiscriminate sex where body and soul are thought to be separate, to open the body is often to open the soul, and vice versa.) Loving is risky because it exposes the inner self, the inner being, the inner identity, making it vulnerable to that other self. And how sad it is if that other self is only manipulating and exploiting the giving self in the name of love.

Nevertheless, to love is to take risks, and the risks, says Klagsbrun, "are enormous, breathtaking, fearsome" (*op. cit.*, p. 21). We take the chance of being crushed by the other's anger or destroyed by the other's laughter. "Yet without that exposure and that honesty between partners," says Klagsbrun, "intimacy cannot exist" (p. 21). If we make ourselves vulnerable will our partner think us worthy or cast us aside?

In today's selfish and exploitative environment it is indeed easy to be cast aside. That is why the commitment to exclusiveness is so important. Closeness depends on a sense that we are unique and special for that one other person, that we share and know each other in ways unavailable to any other person. If others are brought in, trust is diluted and we are fearful of revealing ourselves. It is no wonder the idea of "open marriage" as touted in the '70s was short-lived. Vulnerability to outsiders made trust and intimacy almost impossible for the insiders.

This exclusiveness is firmly supported by the Christian scriptures. Adultery and fornication are condemned. But so are deceitfulness and hardness of heart. In our text Paul advises that we are to stop lying to one another out of fear and greed. We are to do away with covetousness and impurity and slander. Instead, we are to be forgiving and forbearing.

But above all, we are to "put on love, which binds everything together in perfect harmony, " says Paul. Intimacy is not a matter of husband and wife being clones of one another. Rather it means complementarity and compatibility. Intimacy is not an orchestra composed only of violins. Rather it is the different instruments of husband and wife playing harmoniously and fulfillingly.

The love of which Paul speaks means commitment of the will, not just a response to chemistry or emotions. It suggests a lifelong mutuality of deep communications and shared association, histories, children, and memories. It means a love which overcomes the pervasive and insidious loneliness of our time, a love which binds everything together, but in harmony.

Eleanor Rigby, in bridal dress waiting at the church with Father McKenzie, abandoned by someone unwilling to make the commitment for intimacy. "All the lonely people, Where do they all come from?"

They come from unwillingness to take the risks of intimacy.

Prayer

Eternal God, who through Jesus Christ has blessed the world with grace and truth and by whose power has called us anew to a life of faith, hope, and love, we give you thanks for your patience with us and for your determination to bring us to wholeness. We praise you for your decision *before* time to love us *in* time to prepare us for the timelessness of your exhilarating eternity.

By memory and imagination you have enabled us to transcend time, but as creatures of time and sense, and as persons struggling to make sense of the times, we pray that you will draw near to us to help us in our time. Some of us, finding the present unpleasant or distasteful, escape into the nostalgia of the past or into the vain imaginations of the future. Some of us, acutely aware of the passing of time, seek either to arrest it with rigidity or to exploit it with frivolity. Grant us the gift of your wisdom and inspiration that we might make the most of the time.

In these stressful, fretful times, we pray especially for married people, that in the best of times and worst of times their love might grow. In an age when the center cannot hold and things fall apart, grant married people the courage and determination to affirm one another amid diversity rather than abandon one another to perplexity. Help partners to use their differences to grow rather than grouse, to develop rather than divide.

O God of the universe who has chosen to express yourself in the maleness and femaleness of all creation, grant that more and more we might experience the ecstasy and exhilaration of loving you intended for us. Help us to forgive the offenses of the past and to lay aside old grudges as a runner lays aside training weights. Bring us to a new day in our relationships that we might love as you intend us to love.

In the name of Christ we pray. Amen.

Discussion Questions

1. Some see marriage as a threat to true selfhood. Indeed, some (especially women) would claim that marriage and family ruined their chance to actualize true selfhood. Is this true for a lot of people? Does marriage generally enhance or thwart genuine selfhood? How might both marriage and selfhood be enhanced rather than diminished?

2. Some have suggested the new affluence and the economic independence of women have undermined the institution of marriage. If economic necessity once held a marriage together, that is no longer the case. Economically speaking, it is claimed people are much more free to divorce. Do you agree or disagree? How might economic affluence and freedom contribute to a better marriage rather than to divorce?

3. We are told that many people long for intimacy but few achieve it. In today's fast-paced life, what might couples do to achieve a deeper intimacy? What might they avoid doing?

Chapter 10

Morals And Marriage

> *Do you know that your body*
> *is a temple of the Holy Spirit*
> *within you, which you have from*
> *God? You are not your own; you*
> *were bought with a price. So*
> *glorify God in your body.*
> — 1 Corinthians 6:19-20

Let it be admitted from the outset. Speaking about marriage and morality in the same chapter is risky. It is risky because both have been given unfavorable press in recent years. Marriage has been looked upon as a trap, as a boring prison, or as a dull, bourgeois convention.

When driving by a gas station some time ago, I saw one of those portable, electric flashing signs out front. It said in big bold illuminated letters, "Congratulations, Dick. Today you get the ball and chain." Most everyone knew Dick was getting married and that in doing so he was "biting the dust," "getting a ring in his nose," and in general surrendering his male freedom for domiciled domesticity. We were not sure if we should send Dick a card of congratulations or a note of sympathy.

One man, who married in the late 1950s, got the surprise of his life on their wedding night. After the wedding, they were driving through town in a wedding procession, horns honking, cars decorated, with happiness everywhere. He said he was in seventh heaven until, while stopped at a stoplight, a young man yelled out at him, "Sucker!" My friend said it so startled him he wondered if the young man knew something he didn't.

If men of the past thought of marriage as a surrender of freedom, women of more recent times often have regarded marriage as a repressive institution where their selfhood is subordinated to husband and children. Newly liberated by the feminist movement, higher education, and greater participation in the economy, many women look upon marriage as too limiting and circumscribed. That feeling caused one woman to tell her husband, "If you really loved me, you would have married somebody else." So it is, both men and women raise questions about marriage and freedom.

Likewise with morality. The very mention of the word conjures in some minds a grey, dull puritanism or a repressive, mediocre, dull conformity to the mores of a distant past. Morality seems to imply rules, laws, obligations, restrictions, and negation of life and its dynamism, rather than a zesty, vital affirmation of life and participation in its joys. In many ways, both marriage and morality come out rather low on the popularity scale, especially among the young.

Popular or not, we continue to think about marriage and morality, talk about them, worry and wonder about them, as did the ancients and our ancestors. So too, our Christian scriptures, written we believe with the inspiration of the Holy Spirit, address the questions of marriage and morality in various places — not the least of which is Paul's First Letter to the Christians of ancient Corinth.

As many know, Corinth in Paul's time was a wide-open port city in Greece. People came from the world over to indulge in immorality, especially sexual immorality. Consequently, Paul devoted a significant part of his letter to the question of marriage and morality. What advice does the inspired apostle have for us today?

I.

Paul's first bit of advice is that *Christians are to keep body and soul together.*

In Paul's time there was emerging a doctrine called Gnosticism, based on the Greek word *gnosis* which means "to know" in an intimate way. The Gnostics believed knowledge of God was through the mind and spirit and that the body was a hindrance to true communion with God.

The Gnostics accepted the long-standing dualism implicit in much of Greek culture. Dualism believed there were two realities in the world — spirit and matter. Spirit belonged to the High God who was spirit and mind and energy. Matter belonged to a lesser god, the Demiurge. Matter was temporal and decaying, whereas spirit was eternal and life-giving.

In the dualistic view the human spirit was imprisoned in a material body which was a kind of decaying prison house from which the spirit sought to be free. Consequently, the dualists took two extreme views of the body. One view was that of asceticism and discipline. The body was to be brought under complete control so as to serve the human spirit totally.

The other view held that bodily actions had no effect on the spirit whatever. Do whatever you wish in the body. Give expression to its passions and impulses because they have no bearing whatsoever upon the soul or spirit.

The latter view was the more prevalent in ancient Corinth. The dualists had argued that just as food and stomach go together, so do sexual instinct and the body. Both appetites were to be satisfied without thought of marriage or morality. Sexual license or looseness was unrelated to the spiritual life, they argued.

But Paul wrote the Corinthians reminding them that the same Lord who created the human soul or spirit also created the human body. He fashioned the male and female in his image from the dust of the earth and breathed into them the breath of life. The body was no divine accident, nor was it the creation of some lesser god. It was the handiwork of God himself, expressing a totality and unity of spirit and flesh, soul and matter. "The body is not meant for immorality, but for the Lord, and the Lord for the body," wrote Paul in refutation of the dualists. Rather than discarding the body as worthless, God intends to resurrect it and transform it and give it splendor like Christ's resplendent body.

Ironically, in our time, for all our talk of the body and our fascination with it, there has developed a kind of dualism about the body and soul. University of Chicago professor Allan Bloom has made some interesting observations in his best-selling book, *The Closing of the American Mind.* Says Bloom of students today, "... they feel that all sexual acts which do not involve real harm to others are licit. They do not think they should feel guilt or shame about sex" (p. 106).

Students seem to place little value on virginity for themselves or their partners. "For the majority," says Bloom, "sexual intercourse was a normal part of their lives prior to college, and there was no fear of social stigma or even much parental opposition" (*ibid.*). Cohabitation and living together became about as natural as membership in the Girl Scouts.

Of the sexual looseness and cohabitation, one young woman said, "It's no big deal." A young professional woman told me she had no guilt whatever living together with the man who eventually became her husband. Another young woman, to the incomprehension of the older generation, said of the sexual looseness of our time, "What's all the fuss about?" Sexual activity has come to be a normal leisure-time activity, as natural and as morally unencumbered as eating and drinking.

But it isn't as simple as it sounds, says Professor Bloom. What has happened is a kind of separation of body and soul. In making sex easy, "It can trivialize, de-eroticize and demystify sexual relations," says Bloom (*op. cit.*, p. 100). To give the body to another is to make both body and soul vulnerable to the other, to give the other a power over body and soul without loving commitment.

Lest we think only Paul and Professor Bloom feel this way, let us consult the well-known psychoanalyst Rollo May in his best-selling book *Love and Will*. Despite all the increased sexual activity as a result of the sexual revolution, Dr. May says his patients complain of lack of feeling and passion. Internal anxiety has increased in the emphasis on performance, and ironically alienation and loneliness seem to have increased rather than decreased.

Many people today are wary of closeness and intimacy despite the increased sexuality. More and more they treat their body like a machine, says Dr. May. They have divorced emotion and reason amd have separated their souls from their bodies. Many today are inverted Victorians, says the psychoanalyst. "The Victorian person," says Dr. May, "sought to have love without falling into sex; the modern person seeks to have sex without falling into love" (*Love and Will*, p. 46). Consequently there develops a modern dualism or schizoid character against which Paul wrote.

110

But even so liberal and unconventional a thinker as philosopher Bertrand Russell says in his book, *Marriage and Morals*, that romantic love is one of the most intense delights humans can enjoy. And that love, says Dr. Russell, is more than sexuality. There is a longing for affection, for deep intimacy and companionship. Or as he puts it bluntly, "Sex intercourse divorced from love is incapable of bringing any profound satisfaction of instinct" (*Marriage and Morals*, p. 86). To so engage is to separate body and soul, to dehumanize oneself, and ironically to become more lonely rather than less.

Paul urged morality not because he wanted to repress our natural desires nor because he wanted to look upon sexuality as something bad or dirty or disgusting. Quite the contrary. He saw our bodies as beautiful and our sexuality as a part of God's amazing creativity. God's intent is to bring us to the peak of our humanity, to the beauty and wholeness he intends for us. But in doing so, the Creator of our bodies and souls says we should keep them together in moral commitment and passionate involvement.

II.

If body and soul are to be kept together, *so are freedom and responsibility*, says Paul.

Many of the Corinthian Christians had become so excited about Paul's teaching on grace and freedom they thought they could do anything they pleased. People who previously had thought religion was primarily a matter of law-keeping got carried away with the idea that religion was a matter of accepting free grace. Had you been a sinner? God's grace is greater than all our sin. Had you been enslaved to endless numbers of religious laws which only produced guilt and regret? God had forgiven us and released us from irksome rule-keeping as ways of winning God's acceptance.

Consequently, some of the Corinthians were saying to Paul, "All things are lawful for me." Yes, all things may be lawful, says Paul, but not all things are helpful. Besides, once you have given up slavery to law or some other master, it is easy to become enslaved to another. In other words, our newfound liberty can quickly be turned into license. And rather than doing what the law pleases or what the Lord pleases, we do what *we* please.

Once again, Allan Bloom has been very perceptive in his description of the emphasis on individualism and freedom and self-indulgence in our society. He suggests that students today are not "great-souled." "Their primary preoccupation is themselves, understood in the narrowest sense" (*op. cit.*, p. 83). "Country, religion, family, ideas of civilization, all the sentimental and historical forces that stood between cosmic infinity and the individual, providing some notion of a place within the whole, have been rationalized and have lost their compelling force." They know, says Bloom, the truth of Tocqueville's dictum that "in democratic societies, each citizen is habitually busy with the contemplation of a very petty subject, which is himself" (p. 86).

But this is the struggle not just of the young, but of the older generations as well. We too are tempted to look out for good old number one without thought for anyone else, even our spouse. In our historic individualism and insistence on personal freedom, we often change our liberty to license and evade responsibility in pursuing our personal paradise. Yes, "all things may be lawful," but are they helpful, asks Paul. Yes, "all things may be lawful" for the newly liberated Christian, but have we only submitted ourselves to the gods of pleasure or self-indulgence or selfishness?

Sociologist Robert Bellah, in his significant book, *Habits of the Heart*, says that the interplay of freedom and responsibility is important in contemporary marriage. On the one hand, many people are enjoying the freedom of getting out of an oppressive marriage due to relaxed stigma regarding divorce. As one comedian put it, the average man has probably thought twice about running away from home — once as a child and once as a husband! However, on the other hand, they are unsure just where responsibility and commitment leave off and freedom begins.

The same is true in terms of the pursuit of the genuine feeling of love and the sense of obligation. We are torn, says Dr. Bellah, between our craving for an expression of spontaneous inner freedom which seems to be deeply satisfying, and the more permanent commitment which transcends the immediate feelings.

The truth is, our feelings and moods may vary with the weather or our indigestion. To follow our impulses and whims without

112

attention to commitment is dangerous indeed. What may be alluring one day might look quite different on another.

For example, a married man in another city confided in me his temptation toward an affair with a married woman. She was attractive, intelligent, understanding and lovely. Weeks went by and she seemed more alluring and available than ever. But then he went through a minor family crisis where his wife was so steady and beautiful and faithful. It opened his eyes to her in a new way. And what is more, it opened his eyes to the other woman in a new way. He saw more realistically how wrong she would be for him, how their personalities would clash, and how he could not possibly afford her expensive tastes. He was grateful that he had not succumbed to change liberty into license.

That is what Paul asks of us in our marriages — a steady faithfulness, subject not to the vicissitudes of mood swings, but subject to a deep commitment to our partner, body *and* soul. A mere relationship doesn't quite do it, says Alan Bloom. Built on convenience more than passion, a relationship is gray, amorphous, anxious, and tentative. There is always the uneasy feeling that we are being exploited and may just as easily be rejected.

But love, Christian love, is an act of the will. Emotions and feelings are too unstable a base to build and sustain a significant relationship. Even Bertrand Russell says it is not enough just to follow one's own impulses and do as you like. There has to be consistency and continuous effort toward that which is beneficial in the long run, says Russell. A deep human relationship is too important to be left to trivial, momentary impulses.

Says Dr. Russell, "The essence of a good marriage is respect for each other's personality combined with that deep intimacy, physical, mental and spiritual which makes a serious love between man and woman the most fructifying of all human experiences" (*op. cit.*, p. 215). Indeed.

So Paul's word for us, combined with that of Jesus and many contemporary authorities, is this. In marriage, keep body and soul together and do not succumb to dualism. Further, while seeking love and passion, let us not use our Christian liberty for selfish license. Instead, let us use it to be responsible to our Lord who made the body ultimately for himself.

Prayer

Eternal God, who has created the world in beauty and who has fashioned the human body in your image, male and female, we praise you for the gifts of life that everywhere abound. You dazzle us with your infinite display of life-forms, from the octopus to the orangutan, from the mollusk to the monkey, from the jellyfish to the giraffe. In constant amazement we examine one species of life after another, overwhelmed with the infinite complexity of your creative mind and power.

But most of all we give thanks for our human life in which you have focused yourself, imaging yourself in human form and human history, manifesting in the magnificent interplay of masculinity and femininity the mysterious depths of your Being. And when in love we are able to share the powerful union of masculinity and femininity and participate in the procreation of another human life, we are overcome with wonder and awe. We praise you and give you thanks for making us participants in your life and Being.

In your presence it is for us to confess our frequent misuse of the gifts you give us and to acknowledge how far short we fall of the life goals which you have for us and which we have set for ourselves.

If we have over-scheduled ourselves in order to evade ourselves, help us to come to grips with who we are. If we have over committed ourselves, neglecting the spouse and family to whom we should be most committed, help us to see again who is most important in life. If we have been selfish and self-indulgent, insisting always on our own way, give us patience to listen to our loved ones and strength to give to them, rather than expecting always to receive.

Loving, faithful Creator of us all, we confess to you our temptations toward unfaithfulness both to you and our beloved. Save us from the power of vain imaginations and lustful illusions. While we want to be spared from priggish puritanism, so would we be spared from idolatry and greed, lust and infidelity.

O God, rescue us from our bad habits, our self-centeredness, our harmful inhibitions, our fears and frustrations. Release us from age-old conflicts and arguments. Bring us out of stalemate into the glories of love and intimacy, communion and companionship.

In Christ's name we pray. Amen.

Discussion Questions

1. Has the sexual looseness of our time de-eroticized and de-mystified and de-sanctified the sexual experience? Is this good or bad? Was the sexual experience too much exalted in the past? Has it been too much debased in the present? How might Christians today develop an "appropriate" understanding of the sexual experience?

2. It has been said that ours is a narcissistic age. Everyone is in love with himself or herself. Are people today so self-absorbed that it is impossible for them really to love another? If so, how might couples take steps to move out of obsessive self-love to genuine love of the other?

3. Many people regard dictums regarding sexual morality as repressive, stultifying, and unromantic. How would you respond to this criticism? What sexual and marriage moral dictums might be suggested that do not appear to be repressive or unromantic?

Chapter 11

A Candle In The Wind —
A Case For Love And Marriage

*Let marriage be held in honor among
all, and let the marriage bed be
undefiled; for God will judge the
immoral and adulterous.*
— Hebrews 13:4

In one of my churches, it was our custom on Christmas Eve for choir and clergy to process and recess with lighted candles in our beautiful candlelight service. After the serene and reverential "Silent Night" was sung by one of our young choristers, we asked people to leave silently until they reached the outside door.

It had been my custom for those sixteen Christmases I was there to stand at the front door, outside or just inside, to greet the worshipers and wish them a Merry Christmas. As I stood there greeting the radiant faces, I tried to keep my candle lighted, as a symbol of the hope and radiance of the Christ child. Invariably, however, my candle was blown out by the strong winds coming up the hill to the portico and front door.

So it is that the winds of the world seem often to blow out the light of Christ in a darkened age. On Christmas Eve we sing of peace as we have for centuries, but we do so amid the winds of war, our candles flickering and faltering in the turbulence of greed, hate and overambitious power plays.

But nearly every day of the year, we hold forth our lighted candles against the dark winds and furies which would engulf us. We speak for the humanity of man in the midst of gross inhumanity. We speak of forgiveness in a world of grudge-bearing and getting even. We bear witness to grace and graciousness in a society passing law upon law, besieging and oppressing us with more

117

and more legalism. We attempt a word of truth in a time nourished on half-truth and falsehood.

A Jewish friend, visiting our Christmas Eve service, commented on its beauty and inspiration. He then remarked that regrettably he felt we ministers and rabbis were losing the battle. We were but candles in the wind.

But there is an added dimension today, as perhaps there has been in most days. On Christmas Eve I have come to expect the winds *outside* the church to blow out my candle. The real surprise would come if my candle were to be blown out by winds from *inside* the church.

Yet today, it often seems there is as much contrary wind *within* the church as without. A minister can get to feeling like the prophet Elijah long ago, lamenting before God that, I, I alone am left to speak the Word of the Lord. All seem to be against me. Indeed, to press it further, any thinking minister feels the contrary winds raging within his *own* mind and heart. This light for the world of which we speak seems only a candle in the wind — wind *inside* the church as well as outside.

Such is the case with concepts of love and marriage. Not only does our culture advocate varieties of sexual loving relationships outside of marriage; some people within the church seem to argue in a similar way, against the church's historic norms. A recent article in one newspaper indicated that over forty percent of teachers of religion in colleges and universities were not opposed to premarital sex. If soap operas, situation comedies, movies, and novels take it for granted that people bed down together whenever they please, increasing numbers of Christians assume the same. The contrary winds of immorality are stirring inside the hearts of church members as well as in the hearts of those outside the church.

Nevertheless, one of the purposes of worship is to remind ourselves of the morals and values which have been handed down to us from Jesus and the apostles. We worship to gain perspective on ourselves, to ascertain whether the spirit of the times is in harmony with the spirit of our Lord.

Thus, we turn again to the scriptures, to that sacred deposit of our traditions and doctrines and principles, to find the will of the

Lord for our time. More specifically, we need to be reminded of the eternal values which survive the whims and fads and fashions of the passing scene, especially those values which have to do with love and marriage. We do so knowing that for many it may seem but a candle in the wind.

I.

First, let's take a look at a *Christian case for marriage*.

Let it be said that marriage is *in* today in the general culture. That is to say, traditional marriage ceremonies are *in* as well as a few traditional concepts of marriage. I remember well the 1960s and early 1970s when, if young people bothered to marry, they did so in novel ways. In Minneapolis I married a young couple at Minnehaha Falls. Because of a drought, there was little water coming over the falls, except the morning of the wedding it was gushing over. I asked the best man if he knew where the water had come from. He produced a wrench by which he had opened the dam to the holding pond upstream! I was afraid the police would show up any minute.

There were marriages underwater, on horseback, in parachutes, on motorcycles, and in airplanes. One wedding party came down the aisle in a beautiful church wedding, elegantly dressed, but barefoot. We forgot to hang out the familiar sign, "no shirt, no shoes, no service."

Not only were there novel settings for weddings, many couples wanted novel words. Most couples wanted to write their own vows. Some wrote poetry and prayers. Others even wanted to write my wedding sermon! (Modesty was not one of the nobler virtues of that generation!) Nevertheless, today for the most part, the traditional ceremony is very much *in*. However, only recently I had a request from a young man who more or less wanted to stage a major musical as a part of his ceremony. When we suggested he not trivialize such a sacred moment by making it into a show, he decided to go elsewhere. Then I had a new request from a bride who wanted the whole wedding party to leave the church by helicopter. "We want our wedding to be different, to be memorable. We want to, well, give it a lift," she mused.

119

Traditional weddings may now be *in*, but traditional moral values are nearly passé among many. On many college and university campuses, premarital sex is almost as accepted and casual as kissing was a generation ago. Usually by the third date the boy or the girl is suggesting they get "more physical," which doesn't mean more jogging. If an earlier generation was ashamed to come to the marriage bed *without* its virginity, many in the present generation are ashamed to come to the marriage bed *with* their virginity. Apparently today many prefer used, experienced partners to fresh, new ones. Indeed, if today Jesus were to tell the story of the ten virgins, he might have trouble finding examples!

And when you think of it, the church's traditional teaching of love and sex within marriage may seem almost impossible. Just think of the powerful urges at work within us, God-given urges at that. Note again the fantastic transformations of the adolescent years with eros and sexuality, like June busting out all over. The Almighty has made it certain the race will propagate itself, by instinct and impulse if in no other way. With nature itself drawing the sexes toward one another with almost irresistible power, it seems nearly hopeless to suggest restraint and control. In the prime of their lives, we place our young people in colleges and universities where they have maximum sexual temptation and opportunity with minimum restraint or control. With advertising, movies, music, and literature of every kind advocating indiscriminate sexual union, the church's age-old principles must indeed seem like candles in the wind.

Nevertheless, the church's light refuses to go out, much like those trick birthday candles we cannot blow out. The church's witness will not go out because God is behind it and because it represents the *moral* will of God in addition to the *natural* will of eros and sex. The church reminds us we are created not just as erotic bodies with powerful passions. We are also created as persons — minds, spirits, and souls. The church bears witness to the eternal truth that body and soul *are* inextricably bound together. What we do in one affects the other. Casual sex in the body will affect the soul. Self-esteem and a healthy self-image are matters of both soul and body.

Some of us fantasize sexually, but, says philosopher Sam Keen, "The orgy strips away the precise uniqueness of the person that is the basis of romance" (*The Passionate Life*, p. 9). In our time of instant everything, we have tried instant intimacy, says Keen, only to find that it backfires on us and makes us *less* a person rather than *more*.

Dr. Keen goes on to say, "The expectation that uninhibited sex would lessen aggression proved false. Why? Because to reduce communion between persons to contact between bodies, anonymous sex organs, and nerve endings was already an act of violence." Dr. Keen then wisely adds, "The touch that heals always feels and cherishes the other as a unique person" (*ibid.*, p. 18).

It is because we are interested in the *whole* person that we advocate love and sex *within* the commitment of marriage. We are too cynical about the so-called promises of love proffered in the car or motel or dormitory. We parents who have nurtured our sons and daughters from infancy with blood, sweat, and tears think we know something about true love. And we refuse to equate it with the one-night stand or the passionate promise to love each other for at least a semester. We are interested in that young man or woman who will love our sons or daughters as we love them, as a whole person, not just as a sex object to be exploited, even if the exploitation is mutual. If it is true love, then make your commitments in public before God and family and friends. If it isn't true love, why give your sexual self to anything less?

The truth is, married people live longer than single people. Marriage is healthier. So, says Milton Berle, if you're looking for a long life and a slow death, get married!

Nevertheless, singleness can be problematic. One single woman was speaking to me of her loneliness and of her longing to be loved sexually. She spoke of single women friends of hers who, though Christians, were offering their dates that special "dessert" the second or third time out. And she noted they had plenty of dates and she had few. She was wondering if she was too old-fashioned. Perhaps she should loosen up and satisfy those deep longings.

On the other hand, many of those rather indiscriminate persons never really marry the person of their dreams. They often find they have been used and discarded. But some singles of my acquaintance have refused to fool around and in due time were happily married to remarkable persons who held values similar to their own. Namely, they found persons who loved them as a whole person, not just as a sex object for temporary satisfaction of passion.

Yes, I know all this is a candle in the wind, but I believe it to be the Lord's candle. And in the long run, is it not better to go with the eternal principles of our Lord than with the passing fads and fancies, the whims and passions of the present age? As our text says, "Let marriage be held in honor, for God will judge the immoral and adulterous."

II.

But if the church would advocate the importance of marriage, let it also speak up in behalf of *love*.

And first off we must make confession of our narrowness, rigidity, and repression in this area. While we owe an immeasurable debt to Saint Augustine, the great philosopher and theologian, we have inherited from him some unfortunate attitudes toward the body and sex. As is well known, Saint Augustine was a Manichaean for a time, embracing their dualistic notion that the body was evil and that only the spirit was good. Some of those notions carried over into his Christian days and introduced a negative attitude toward the body and sex.

Go farther back in history to Saint Paul in his First Letter to the Corinthians (Chapter 7), and he seems to give sex, love, and marriage a second place compared to his own celibacy. Thus, in due time, celibacy became the standard for priests, monks, and nuns in the western church. Marriage was regarded as a lesser mode of existence, a bit beneath the higher spirituality of the single, celibate life.

Closer to our time we have had to contend with the Victorian notions of sex and body. Actually, the Puritans had a rather healthy attitude toward sexuality. It was the Victorians who tended toward prudery and dualism. Thus the church with its lingering dualism and Victorianism has to take its share of the blame for unhealthy inhibitions and repressions regarding love and sex.

122

That said, let us go on to affirm the body as the joyful creation of God. The Genesis story tells us that our maleness and femaleness are the expression of God's image. When Adam beholds Eve standing before him in the altogether, he exclaims, "This at last is bone of my bones, and flesh of my flesh," which is a rough primordial equivalent of the modern "WOW!" And so it has been ever since. For most people the body of the opposite sex has been fantastically alluring and attractive. Mark Twain certainly understood that. He once was asked, "In a world without women, what would men become?" Twain replied, "Scarce, sir, mighty scarce."

Most of us carry a mild cynicism toward those so-called platonic relationships. Whatever else we may be, we surely are body — sexual bodies with all the drives, desires, and passions. Let no one assign such beautiful powers to the Devil. As always, it is the Devil who *distorts* and *perverts* such powers.

Therefore many married couples need to reawaken those powers and drives as a way of renewing the love bond between them. Many marriages have grown dull and stale because partners have ignored or neglected themselves as bodies. Some allow lack of grooming and hygiene or poor body habits to impede the physicality of their relationship. Some still have Victorian notions of sex as dirty or animalistic. Others in marriage have become preoccupied with careers and jobs and hobbies to the neglect of each other. Still others have made their marriage an ongoing argument. But they need to be reminded of Abraham Lincoln's wry observation that "no matter how much cats fight, there always seem to be plenty of kittens."

Once again we turn to Sam Keen, who observes: "We misunderstand love because we have chosen to worship power; we fail in compassion because we have become obsessed with control; we silence the reasons of the heart because we have chosen to follow a path of heartless knowledge ..." (*op. cit.*, p. 4).

How easy it is for people to become obsessed with careers at the expense of love. Remember the book, *The Thorn Birds*, and the television series based on the book? I was able to catch bits and pieces of the television novel. In the final episode, Father Ralph, now a Cardinal in the Roman Catholic Church, returns to his Australian homeland, where he dies. In the closing scenes, he is speaking with Meggie, with whom he was always in love and by whom he fathered a child.

However, Father Ralph, now Cardinal Ralph, always claimed he loved God more than Meggie, and that therefore he could never marry her. But now, in the touching and dramatic closing scenes, he says to her that she was always able to choose to love, in spite of the tragedies which befell her. And how about himself? "I see now," says Ralph, " that it was not my love of God that kept me from you, but my love of myself. It was my ambition to be a Cardinal of the church that kept me from choosing love. O Meggie, will you forgive me this terrible wrong that I have visited upon you?" he pleads. And then in the radiance of that self-revelation and the tenderness of that powerful, loving moment, he dies. And once again, Megan has lost one whom she dearly loved — lost to the powerful grip of ambition.

Ralph's story grips us because it often is our story — a story of love short-changed by ambition, a story of tenderness overcome with greed, a story of would-be intimacy replaced by the compulsion to make a name for ourselves. When the truth is known, many of us are willing to lose our souls for the sake of gaining the world, no matter how small and crumbling and transitory that world might be.

As Dr. Edwin Johnson has said, "Our sexuality, far from being a distraction from God, can be understood as the instrument by which God created us and continues to manifest himself to us" *In Search of God in the Sexual Underworld*, p. 163). Dr. Johnson goes on to say that "the flesh is the mode of creation. God's love for us and our love for God is experienced in our flesh" (*ibid.*, pp. 163-164). Therefore, says Dr. Johnson, "a positive attitude toward sex can help bring us into touch with the resurrected body we carry so unconsciously along with us all our lives" (*ibid.*, p. 164). In a similar vein, Bishop Fulton Sheen has said love is not an ascent from the animal world, but a descent from God to be expressed in our bodies.

In a time when many marriages suffer from boredom, dullness, stalemate, and hostility, these principles and morals may seem indeed like a candle in the wind. But we believe it to be God's candle. After all, he created us male and female. And he designed us to experience him, to express his image in the delights of conjugal, married love. As Christians, we have been raised up with Christ to regard our bodies and sex and love in this new creative way. We are his workmanship, created for good deeds, one of which surely is to celebrate the wonder and mystery of devoted, married love.

The words of our text are still eternally true:

> *Let marriage be held in honor among all,*
> *and let the marriage bed be undefiled;*
> *for God will judge the immoral and adulterous.*

Prayer

Loving Father of the universe, who has chosen to manifest your image in the maleness and femaleness of humanity upon planet earth, and who has again, in the very person of Jesus, revealed your love and will and person: praise be to you not only for your power which creates and sustains all, but for your love and compassion which give meaning to all. We gather in awe of your majesty, but we are bold to approach you, confident by your mercy that we will find grace in our time of need.

O Lord God, we believe you have placed us in the world for love, and we can only confess our repeated failures. From Adam and Eve to the present, we have turned aside, each to his own, ignoring you and neglecting our brother. In the anxiety of living and the fear of being vulnerable, we have drawn into ourselves and have grasped the things of time and sense to make us secure. In our defensiveness with our calculating selfish hearts, we have sought always to get more out of relationships than we give. Forgive, O Lord, our mean-spiritedness and smallness of heart.

O God, source of all our life and love, you have asked us to live in cooperation with you and to present our needs to you as heart to heart. Be pleased then to hear our requests for our young people. Grant that they might learn to treat their bodies as temples of your

125

Holy Spirit. As they come into the full bloom of their sexuality, give them the power of self-control, so that the celebration of love and union may be within the bonds of married commitment. Save them from exploitation, from disease, from the broken heart which comes from being used and then abandoned. In this highly erotic age, give them strength to resist the temptations which everywhere abound. Grant, O Lord, that they might be whole, celebrating the wonder of their maleness and femaleness in the commitment of marriage.

O Lord, we pray for those with special needs; for husbands and wives whose marriages have grown boring and stale, that they might be awakened again to the power and wonder of love; for those divorced or divorcing, that they might open a new chapter on life and recover a wholeness lost or never found; for the elderly, often widowed, that their life might be filled with purpose and friendships; for those confused about their sexuality and about love, that your will for them might become clear; for children and others sexually abused, and that this horrendous wrong might stop, and these terrible wounds be healed. See, O Lord, how great is our need of you and your loving power. Heal us, we pray, with that perfect love which casts out all fear.

Through Jesus Christ our Lord. Amen.

Discussion Questions

1. In today's culture when many young people are at work or away at college at the peak of their sexual powers, is it unrealistic to expect they will remain chaste or celibate until marriage? With couples marrying later and later, waiting until they are "financially secure," is it unrealistic to expect them not to live together? What alternative ways of thinking and acting might Christians suggest? Or should the prevailing popular standards be embraced as good?

2. It is said that many people today are ambitious for success, so much so that marriage is seen only as an adjunct to the career path. Would you agree? Disagree? Should marriage and family be primary or secondary to career? Why? Why not?

3. In your view, do the majority of Christians today agree with the prevailing notions of sexual morality where sex and commitment are separated? Is sexual intercourse to the present generation what kissing and necking were to previous generations? What might Christians suggest as appropriate dating behaviors for today?

Chapter 12

Marriage –
The Long And Short Of It

Love knows no limit to its endurance,
no end to its trust,
no fading of its hope,
it can outlast anything.
It is, in fact,
the one thing that still stands
when all else has fallen.

— 1 Corinthians 13:8
(Phillips translation)

Probably one of the best forms of entertainment still available for free is people-watching. It can be fun and instructive to sit in a restaurant or an airport or train station, sit in a shopping mall, or stand on a street corner to watch people. The clothes they wear, the hairdos and make-up, the gait and stance all suggest a life-story — intriguing perhaps, even mysterious.

Sometimes by watching couples — either lovers or married partners — you can get an idea of the nature of their relationship. Or watch them in their cars or at social gatherings. Sometimes it's clearly a situation of "if looks could kill." On such occasions it's a good idea not to come between them. You might receive the lightning bolt of hostility intended for the spouse or partner. Policemen involved in settling domestic disputes know something about that.

If people-watching is fascinating, so is people-listening. Sometimes we can learn so much by overhearing conversations. For example, on the train the other morning, a married man was talking to a single man. "My wife keeps telling me that she gave me the best years of her life. If those were the best, now I have to worry about what we've got coming up!" With an increased audience, he

129

went on to say, "Ah, yes, we've been happily married for ten years. Ten out of thirty isn't bad!"

In the next car two women were exchanging opinions on love and marriage. One said to the other, "My friend just gave her husband a divorce because he was in love with himself, and she didn't want to stand in the way! Ah, yes," she continued, "I read that one marriage out of three ends in divorce. The other two fight it out to the bitter end. I guess we've been married so long because of our compatibility — we both love to fight."

But then she got quieter and more personal and said, "Confidentially, I would divorce my husband tomorrow if I could figure out a way to do it without making him happy!"

Well, does divorce make us happy?

A few years ago I came across a former parishioner in another city. Upon asking about her health and husband, she said, "Bob and I are divorced now." "Oh, I'm sorry," I said in instinctive reaction. "Don't be sorry," she said. "It's the best thing that ever happened to me. I've never been happier."

For some people, possibly, divorce does open the way to greater happiness. But in my questionnaires sent to many married couples, I asked how they felt about the high rate of divorce. "Would you," I asked, "recommend divorce as a good way out of a marital difficulty?" And most of them said in one way or another, "Divorce is not a good resort, but a last resort" — a last resort when all else fails.

To be sure, many allowed for divorce in cases of physical or psychological abuse. Many agreed that sometimes spouses are indeed emotionally incompatible. One man wrote: "I think divorce is a good way out. How awful it feels to wake up next to someone you don't love or even like." (I do not think his comment was autobiographical!) But for the most part, the respondents felt that divorce today was too easy, and too quickly used as a solution to difficulties and strife in marriage.

In other words, if we were to ask, "Is marriage for the long haul or the short," they would answer, "for the long." Hang in there. Stick it out. Things will get better, most would say.

I.

Well possibly. But how about the *short of it*? *Cannot something be said* about the *immediacy* of *passion* and the *spontaneity* of *feeling*?

Was that not in many ways the message of the '60s and '70s generation, the "now" generation and the "me" generation? Were they not the generations of sexual liberation and sexual revolution, the Woodstock generation of spontaneity and immediacy, the back-to-the-earth, back-to-the-sensuous, back-to-the-passions-and-feelings generation?

Yes, it was these generations who threw off the prudery of their Victorian parents to get in touch with their bodies and feelings. These were the days of encounter groups and Esalen-type institutes, sitting in mixed nude company in hot tubs getting in touch with ourselves and each other in non-repressed, non-sublimated ways.

These were the days of free love and troikas of one man and two women, or one woman and two men; the days of free love communes where all partners were to be shared without possessiveness or jealousy, and where children, if any, were to be raised by the group. Sociologists of those days were predicting with seriousness that free-love arrangements such as these were the wave of the future, and that soon monogamous, nuclear families would be a thing of the past.

Soon after that, marriage counselors Nena and George O'Neill wrote a book titled *Open Marriage*, advocating a mutually agreed upon end of fidelity. Monogamy can become stale and boring or hostile and embittered. Therefore, might it not be better to allow your spouse to be intimate with other people, asked the O'Neills. After all, it will enrich one's life with variety and may well indeed save the marriage. (Never mind that skeptics at the time scoffed, "save the marriage for what?")

And say what you will about those times, they had a great impact on our understanding of love and marriage. Yes, it is true that out of fear of AIDS the sexual revolution has slowed down somewhat. Yet despite the fact that other sexually transmitted diseases are at epidemic proportions, extramarital and premarital activity remain

131

high — reaching down to high school and even to youngsters only slightly into puberty.

And it is the rare person today who is still a virgin when he or she marries. Indeed, they are almost ashamed to admit virginity. Besides, the majority of people who marry today, for the first or second or third time, have already been living together before the wedding day.

Despite all the possible negatives of the sexual revolution of the "now" generation, the "me" generation, and the "me right now" generation (and there are many), those generations did make incisive critiques of many of our marriages and relationships.

If the truth be known, some of us actually looked at them with envy — envy of the freedom, the spontaneity, the carefree ways, the sensuality and sensuousness we secretly longed for and they seemed to experience easily, casually, freely.

If the truth be known, many of us had let our marriages become largely a practical and economic arrangement "for better or for worse," largely for worse, in our determination, to be sure it would be "richer" rather than "poorer." With hangover Victorianism and repressed libidos, we sublimated our passions for the sake of production, and Puritanically postponed all our pleasures until all the duties of today and tomorrow were done. And since they were never done, we tended toward that Puritan whom Mark Twain described as meanly envious of that fact that someone somewhere might actually be having a good time.

Disciplined by two world wars and a devastating depression, many of the older generation were totally future-oriented, believing that if any real pleasure was to be had, it would be in some distant tomorrow. So we were highly vulnerable to the flower children and hippie-love — vulnerable in our repressed passions to the immediacy and spontaneity and emotional honesty of the temporary moment of the "now" generation.

Yes, that was the short of it — the experience of the now moment, the passionate moment. And who of us does not feel from time to time the powerful drive of erotic desire and the seductive lure of lust and the seemingly liberating pull of unrestrained passion for that one who, for the moment, has captivated our soul.

132

II.

Marriage — the short of it? Yes, there is something to be said for it. But that's not all there is to be said for it. There's also the *long of it* — marriage for the long haul, marriage for the difficult days as well as the easy, marriage for the worse, the poorer, the sickness as well as for the better, the richer, the health.

If the younger generation could rightfully critique the older for lack of spontaneity and immediacy, the older could rightfully critique the younger for lack of continuity and durability. If the younger generation could disdain the older for "grit-your-teeth-and-hang-on-to-hope-for-a-better-tomorrow," the older generation could rightfully level changes of cavalier flippancy and fickle fidelities at the younger.

And if you were to ask yourself where the Bible comes down on the issue of marriage, we would have to say it advocates marriage for the long haul — but marriage with passion and feeling and intimacy, nevertheless.

In his excellent book, *Love and Will*, the late psychoanalyst Rollo May says that the Victorian hoped to fall into love without falling into sex, but that the hippie and flower-child hoped to fall into sex without falling into love. The immediacy and spontaneity of love of the "now" generation was great, said Dr. May, but it often was ephemeral and fugitive.

Ironically and tragically, says Dr. May, with his patients, the more sexually promiscuous they were, the lonelier they became. And they became lonelier, because the motel "short order sex" (as John Galbrath labelled it), did not really involve the will, the self, the person. Strangely and ironically one of the most personal of all human activities became impersonal. And the very act intended to promote deep communication and intimacy actually separated us because, said Dr. May and others, there was no commitment.

When we assume that the ultimate goal of existence is the satisfaction of the impulses, we are led into a *cul-de-sac* of tedium and banality, says Dr. May, and we soon find we have trivialized one of the most sacred aspects of our humanity.

Therefore, say May and others, we need to involve the will, the decision-making center, the center which says I care about you,

133

you are important, you are a fulfillment of my personality and I am resolved to love you in the bad times as well as the good. What is love, asks psychiatrist M. Scott Peck in his best-selling book, *The Road Less Traveled*. Love, says Dr. Peck, "is the will to extend one's self for the purpose of nurturing one's own or another's spiritual growth" (p. 81). "Love is as love does," says Peck. "Love is an act of will — namely, both an intention and an action" (p. 83).

By itself, the romantic love of passionate immediacy and sexual spontaneity are never quite enough for the long haul. Passion at full flame is truly wonderful, but passion as wildfire is truly dangerous and often destructive.

A Chicago divorce attorney, Herbert Glieberman, tries to keep marriages together and has written a book titled *Closed Marriage* and subtitled *Almost Always You Marry the Right Person*. Marriage is hard work, says Glieberman, just as many pointed out in their questionnaires. "Marriage is no sprint that lasts for a week or a month. Marriage is a marathon," says Glieberman. It's not a 100-yard dash, but a long-distance run.

To be sure, some people just stay together to torture one another. But some people stay together because they know down deep that in the arguments, in the disagreements, in the disputes and confrontations, and in the joys and ecstasies, they have come to a greater and deeper and richer truth about themselves; and that through it all they have become much more compassionate and mature, much more resilient and reliable, much more insightful and wise.

Thomas Edison's assistant once said, "It looks like we failed." "Failed," Edison countered. "We're that much closer to success. Now we know fifty ways it can't be done — there can only be a few more wrong ways left. Once we do them, we'll find the right one." And he did.

It is true, of course, that in the last analysis some marriages will just not work. People often marry for the wrong reasons, or find after professional help that they are seriously incompatible, or that the relationship is hopelessly abusive. Sometimes divorce is better, but usually marriage is better.

One lady called to ask if I married people who had been divorced and I answered yes, but that I liked to consult with them beforehand. "Do you marry people who have been divorced more than once?" she asked. "Sometimes," I replied. "Well, I've been divorced seven times," she said. And I said, "Sorry, Elizabeth Taylor, I don't think I can do it, even if you are old-fashioned and believe in marriage. Let's talk it over!"

Is marriage intended to be for the long haul? Indeed it is, even the second marriage or third. But not just for the sake of longevity. T.S. Eliot tells the story of a man who worked fifty years at a job he didn't like, in a company he didn't respect. And at the end, they gave him a gold watch, which he accidentally scratched only to discover it was brass. Marriage and its process should be more than mere unhappy endurance to the end for a golden anniversary that turns out to be brass.

But on the other hand, love and marriage should be something more than immediacy and spontaneity, something more than the passion of the moment and the whimsy of the one-night stand or affair. A few years ago, Carole King put it well for her generation, the "now" generation, when she sang soulfully:

> Tonight you're mine completely.
> You give your love so sweetly:
> Tonight the light of love is in your eyes.
>
> Is this a lasting treasure,
> Or just a moment's pleasure?
> Can I believe the magic of your sigh?
>
> Tonight with words unspoken,
> You say that I'm the only one,
>
> But will my heart be broken
> When the night meets the morning sun?
>
> Will you still love me tomorrow?*

135

And if we love as God loves, we will answer, yes, I'll still love you tomorrow, because as Paul says, "Love knows no limit to its endurance, no end to its trust, no fading of its hope, it can outlast anything. It is, in fact, the one thing that still stands when all else has fallen."

And today, can you say to your beloved, "I will love you with that kind of love"?

May God help it to be so.

Prayer

Eternal God, sustainer of the universe and our sustainer, who has made a world of both freedom and destiny, and who has shaped us with liberty to shape our own lives, praise be to you for choices within the structures of the cosmos, and thanks be to you for your patience with us, as we learn our way in the complexities of human living and loving.

And it is for the loving we especially give thanks. Your impulse of eternal love was felt through our parents and grandparents, our uncles and aunts, brothers and sisters and friends, through teachers and ministers, and sometimes even strangers, who were good Samaritans on life's sometimes torturous way.

In your presence, Almighty God, we are newly aware of how much we have been given that we did not deserve, and of how much we have received that we did not achieve. Forgive our age-old propensity to take the good for granted and to complain over the bad. Wean us from the spoiled-child syndrome, which takes and takes, never learning to give, never learning to have the thankful, gracious heart.

We bring before you today the marriages and families of the church and community and nation. We fear that the most basic social institution of our civilization is coming unglued, being fractured by the forces of greed, and overwhelmed by the rapacious powers of lust. Almighty God, be pleased to bring us all to repentance, to change our ways, to amend our willfulness and selfishness, so that wholeness and health, civility and stability, might invade our land again.

Look with favor upon all broken hearts and troubled minds. For those stressed out by demanding work and fractious marriages, for those with wayward children or arbitrary and hurtful parents, for those alone and so much in need of a dearly beloved, for those enticed by lust and tempted toward the pleasures of the moment over against the rewards of the long haul, for those nearly at the end of their rope and needing a lift from your power and grace, for those bruised by life and neglected by friends, for those too arrogant for true humanity and too prideful for true religion — for all in need, known and unknown, we raise our earnest prayers to you, loving Father, knowing that you care, and that you hear and answer. Be pleased then to answer our plaintive cries, spoken and unspoken.

Through Jesus Christ our Lord. Amen.

Discussion Questions

1. Previous generations, it has been said, repressed their passions and emotions for the sake of duty and success. They were "future-oriented" rather than "now-oriented." Sexuality was sublimated to the work ethic. Do you agree with these observations? Why? Why not? Is the present generation too casual about sex, too insistent on immediate gratification and instant pleasure? If so, is this good or not good? Is there a balance between the two points of view?

2. Some couples have become so accustomed to fighting that this is the only way they can relate. In the fighting, they are at least expressing emotion and caring. As "intimate enemies" they are at least relating, say some. Is this better than not talking at all? Is it better to fight than to be silent or indifferent? What advice to improve their relationship might be given to couples in perpetual verbal conflict?

3. From time to time it is suggested that an affair might be good for a marriage, to eliminate boredom, to add spice to the marriage, and to forestall divorce. What do you think of such advice? Could "open marriage" be good for a marriage? Why? Why not?

Chapter 13

Stalemates, Soulmates, Lifemates

> *Put on then, as God's chosen ones,*
> *holy and beloved, compassion, kindness,*
> *lowliness, meekness, and patience,*
> *forbearing one another and,*
> *if one has a complaint against another,*
> *forgiving each other;*
> *as the Lord has forgiven you,*
> *so you also must forgive.*
>
> — Colossians 3:12-13

It's one of my favorite stories. An older couple was celebrating their fiftieth wedding anniversary. Their children had made elaborate arrangements for a dinner party at the club. The food had been terrific, the music excellent, and the reminiscences and testimonials touching and humorous.

As the festivities began to wind down, the husband leaned over to his hard-of-hearing wife of fifty years and said, "Honey, I'm proud of you." She said, "What did you say?" He said, "Honey, I'm proud of you." Quizzically she asked again, "What?" Raising his voice he repeated, "I said I'm proud of you." And she said, "That's okay, I'm tired of you too!"

If it took fifty years for that couple to come to weariness with each other, no doubt many couples would say it has taken far less time for them to become tired of each other. For some married people, it takes only a few short years to settle into a tired routine, and to resign themselves to a relationship of cool indifference.

Even their arguments become old hat. She has heard for the thousandth time that she has the same bad habits of her mother, and she has assured him in no fewer times that he is repeating the same annoying behavior so characteristic of his father.

She says he is hypercritical, is self-righteous, is wrapped up in himself, and is a poor listener. He says she is oversensitive, and cannot be satisfied with anything less than perfection, and that that means perfection according to her definitions.

She says he is never home, that he thinks far more of his job and career than of her and the family, and that he is insensitive to her and arbitrary and unfeeling with the children. He says she doesn't appreciate how hard he works to be successful in a cut-throat world, so as to provide her and the children with the kind of lifestyle to which they have become accustomed.

And she says she now has a job and career of her own to worry about, and that he can take a little more responsibility for the children, and cooking, and housework, and that he doesn't really appreciate how much money she is bringing into the situation. And he says he feels like he doesn't have a wife anymore, but a kind of financial partner who has lost her charm, and her capacity really to listen to him and the children.

And when they are older, she says, she needs to have a job and other interests, because now that the children are gone, we don't have much in common anymore, and that she finds life more interesting outside the home and marriage. And he says that he was thinking of retiring early so he could travel and do things they never had time to do before, but that now she is tied down to a job she financially really doesn't need. And she tells her friends that retirement is that part of life when you have twice as much husband and half as much money!

If the truth be known, probably many of us would say our marriages and relationships get bogged down in stalemated arguments or resigned hostilities which have gone on for years. One older couple of my acquaintance started arguing about money the day they were married and, as far as I could tell, were still having the same argument up to the day they died. They proved again and again the truth of that ancient witticism, that if it weren't for marriage, we would have to fight with perfect strangers!

But, we might ask, is there not a way to move out of these tired, circular, stalemated arguments? Is there not a way out of repressed anger and masked hostility to enjoy the exhilaration and enrichment of a soulmate and lifemate?

Paul, the great apostle, points us in the right direction in this popular text of Colossians. Christians, says Paul, should not continually grovel around in old, destructive, boring patterns of behavior. Instead, they are to be "raised from the dead," so to speak, resurrected, revitalized and transformed, so as to experience life on a higher level. "Seek those things which are above, where Christ is," says Paul.

He then adds we are to put off old behavior patterns and put on new ones. Get out of the old, smelly, moth-eaten, psychological garments of the past, and put on the new, fresh, fashionable, spiritual, psychological garments of the new you and the new marriage you can become.

I.

So first Paul says, *Take it off, take it all off.*

Take off what, we might ask? In Paul's words, do away with "fornication, impurity, passion, evil desire, and covetousness, which is idolatry." In short, we might call these behaviors those of greed and selfishness. Fornication, impurity, and passion are attitudes of sexual selfishness, wherein one or both partners use the other for sexual gratification, without personal involvement or commitment.

The Greek words Paul uses here suggest uncontrollable desire much like that expressed in marauding armies, raping, pillaging, and destroying everything in their path. The words suggest the uncontrolled wanderings of wild horses running and rampaging by influence of impulse alone.

But perhaps the most telling Greek word used by Paul is *pleonexia*, which suggests a ruthless grasping and groping to possess and control everything, including one's spouse. It can include the proverbial dominating husband, to the proverbial manipulating wife.

Pleonexia, sometimes translated "covetousness" but perhaps better translated "ruthless greed," is used by Plato to denote the ruthless tyrant, the person who will pursue his or her own selfish interests regardless of the costs to others. For the Greek moralists, it was the worst of the antisocial sins — *pleonexia*, a greedy, grasping selfishness.

141

In my questionnaire sent to many married couples I asked, "What in your opinion are the three most serious problems married couples face today?" One problem mentioned many times centered around money, two-career marriages, and competitiveness. Many did not feel that two-career families were necessarily wrong, but that the added stress, the potential rivalry and competitiveness, and the pressure to make lots of money could be troublesome.

One woman said that the problem was a lack of free time, where everything is in a rush, busy, "scheduled," so that it seems you have to make an appointment to spend quality time with your husband and children. Added to that the financial pressures, the cost of living, education, child-rearing, "the mortgage," and striving always to have the best, do put great pressures on us.

Her husband added that the prevailing selfish attitudes, the unrealistic expectations, the loss of traditional values, and two-income families which may contribute to a lack of interdependency can add to marital difficulties.

We might ask ourselves, "How much is enough?" Most of us would say it is admirable to work hard, to achieve, and to be successful. Most of us prefer success to failure, although failure can bless us in strange sorts of ways. But to be obsessive-compulsive, to be possessed by a greedy heart and rapacious mind, will surely lead at least to a stalemated marriage and relationship, if indeed not a hostile one.

So give it up, says Paul. Take it off. Put to death the *pleonexia* within you. Learn to relax into the grace of God and, we might add, learn to relax into the grace, and beauty, and wonder of your partner. Instead of "possessing" and "dominating" the partner, how about liberating the partner from our obsessive need to control, and thereby be free to celebrate who he or she really is, in place of what we are trying to make that person be.

But Paul also suggests we put away some other spiritual-psychological styles which have become destructive. Do away with malice, wrath, anger, slander, obscene talk, and lying to each other. As in all human relationships, so in marriage, anger and lying can lead to stultifying stalemates.

So how do we go about getting rid of anger? Not by denying it, not by repressing it, not by sublimation, not by excessive internalization. No, not by those spiritually and psychologically crippling techniques. Rather, to move beyond stalemates to soulmates anger must be recognized, admitted, and properly expressed.

In their book, *Lifemates*, Harold Bloomfield and Sirah Vettese say that "an irony of love is that it guarantees some degree of anger. When two people fall in love, they expose the most sensitive parts of their personalities. At some time in every love relationship, lovers are inconsiderate, hurt each other's feelings, or let each other down. Anger is the natural result, and to keep love vibrant, the anger must be expressed" (p. 119). They go on to add that "when resentments accumulate, emotional defenses harden and feelings of love wither" (*ibid.*).

Anger is a way to get attention. Anger is a way of saying you have been deeply hurt by your beloved. Anger is a way of saying "I am somebody" and you have been ignoring me or hurting me. Anger is a way of saying you are not loving me. Anger can be the anguished cry for love. So instead of turning the anger inward to lead to psychosomatic ailments, or turning it outward to abuse and violence, we need to learn to express anger in our relationships. So how, we might ask.

Bloomfield and Vettese suggest we should avoid the "I'm right, you're wrong trap." We all can be incredibly self-righteous. Further, say the authors, "There is always a Greek chorus of like-minded friends and relatives who unequivocally support how right you are and obviously wrong your lover is" (*ibid.*, p. 14). We need to remember that our legitimate anger does not always mean our partner is wrong.

Further, in expressing anger, avoid win/lose arguments where it is a struggle to develop the best putdown. Move beyond either/or situations. Life is usually too complex for simplistic views. Avoid arrogant assumptions about your partner that presume you know better what he or she is thinking or feeling.

Avoid alcohol and times of excessive stress when expressing anger. Try to have the presence of mind to suggest a cooling-off period or a "time-out" until you are more rested and the combative effects of too much alcohol have dissipated. Set an agreeable time and pleasant place, free of distraction, in which to express your anger.

Some people become verbally vicious in anger, but they and we have to learn not to hit below the belt with gross generalizations, with demeaning accusations, and remarks meant only to sabotage the other. Lighten up a little. Do as one couple told me in the questionnaire they do, and that is add some hilarity and humor. Ease off a little. Remember that your anger at bottom is probably a plea for love and understanding. So express it, get it out in as positive a way as possible, and the anger expressed can have transforming power.

II.

How do we move from stalemates to soulmates to lifemates? It is a matter not only of putting off bad, old, psychological-spiritual habits. It is also a matter of putting on some new ones, says Paul.

Listen to the list again: Put on compassion, kindness, forbearance, and forgiveness. You should forgive as the Lord has forgiven you, says Paul. And above all, put on love, which binds everything together in harmony, and be thankful. Whew! That's a tall order, isn't it?

However, in the beautifully thoughtful responses many gave in their questionnaires, they said many of the same things. Many said that taking each other for granted was one of the problems in marriage, which is another way of saying we have ceased to be thankful for each other.

They added that marriage is "hard work" but that it is worth it. One man said, "I've been happily single and I am happily married, and I can report that happily married is happily better. All of those (statements) so often used that they've become corny, statements about sharing and caring and fulfilling, are really true." He continues: "Having someone to love, who you know loves you in return, to share your life with, sharpens the view, brightens the colors, sweetens the taste, and lengthens the laughter."

Many respondents would agree, but would add that to make that kind of marriage happen we must learn to communicate. What are some of the serious problems in marriage, I asked. And almost all of the respondents said communication, communication, communication. And what would help in solving marital problems, I asked. Communicate, communicate, communicate, they replied.

Psychiatrist Paul Tournier would agree. "No one can develop freely in this world and find full life without feeling understood by at least one person," says Tournier (*To Understand Each Other*, p. 25). Indeed, one of the deepest hungers of the heart is to be understood and accepted. But to be properly understood, we must learn to communicate with kindness, compassion, humility, forbearance, and forgiveness. We need to be at least "friends."

Some marriages have come to the point where fighting seems to be the chief recreation, and the function of the hostility seems to be that of allowing touching without intimacy. The great Russian novelist Dostoevski asks, what is hell? "I maintain it is the suffering of being unable to love." And being unable to love is often linked to our inability to communicate.

So how then should we communicate? Most couples spend less than thirty minutes a week sharing their most intimate feelings, say Vettese and Bloomfield. If people continue to hide or suppress their deepest feelings, the relationship is doomed to boredom and chronic frustration.

Therefore, Vettese and Bloomfield suggest the "Tell Me More" technique for good communication. When your spouse or lover or friend begins to express anger, frustration, or hostility, a positive technique is simply to say, "Tell me more," which is another way of saying we need to have enough kindness and compassion for our partner to be a good listener. We talk past one another, with no one receiving — really receiving what is said.

Think of the disarming words from a spouse who says, "Tell me more." Really? You really want to hear more, we say in disbelief. And the partner says in a kindly, non-sarcastic way, "Tell me more," and so gradually we do tell more and more and gradually our frustrations begin to ease, our muscles begin to relax, the tension in our face fades, and we begin to believe we've been "heard."

Not necessarily "agreed with" but "heard." With forbearance and kindness our partner listened and we spoke. Our partner, kindly and in a non-accusatory way, asked, do you mean this or that, and then we could further explicate our feelings. And in doing so, we begin to feel loved and appreciated because we were heard.

"Communication fails," say Vettese and Bloomfield, "because you become so involved in defending yourselves, trying to control each other and proving you are 'right' that you can't hear what each really needs" (*ibid.*, p. 38).

"Tell me more. I see you are upset. Why don't you relax with a cold drink and tell me more about your day?" When you do that, can't you just feel yourself biting your tongue and starting to become defensive when your partner expresses anger and criticism? Overcome the urge to counterattack. Look him or her in the eyes and say sincerely, "Tell me more."

Do it when you have time. Be patient. Don't interrupt. Don't jump to conclusions. Try to get the whole story. Tell me more, you say with sincere compassion and empathy. Withhold judgment and accusations. Accept your partner's point of view without the compulsion to set him or her right. Give your sincere, undivided attention in an effort to understand. And don't be worried now about "equal time." Your time will come. In humility and thoughtfulness say, "Tell me more." This can be a big step from being stalemates to becoming soulmates.

So how will it be if we live long enough to celebrate a fiftieth wedding anniversary? Will we have been married to several different spouses by that time? Or if we have been married to the same person, will we in fact be "tired of him or her"?

Not, says Paul, if we put off the old spiritual-psychological traits which lead to destruction. And not if we put on the new spiritual-psychological traits of compassion, kindness, and sharing. We can indeed move from stalemates to become deeply enriched soulmates, committed to being lifemates, *"till death do us part."*

Prayer

Almighty God, Lord of the universe, who dwells in mystery, incomprehensible to the human mind, transcending all categories of thought and systems of belief, by your grace you have manifested yourself in all the created world, and have left your imprint in the hearts and minds of prophets and apostles, and finally in Jesus Christ. We praise and adore you for helping us to think your thoughts after you, and for allowing us to participate in your Being, as the swimmer participates in the ocean. We gather in this sacred place and sacred time to declare our love for you and to beseech your assistance in our love for one another.

We must confess in your presence our difficulty in loving. The lofty ideals we embrace in worship or on wedding days seem too easily defeated in the sometimes harsh realities of everyday living. The hopes and aspirations of our dreaming innocence too often are overcome by misunderstanding, rejection, and outright hostility. Forgive us, loving Father, for our many times of failing to be what we know we should be and want to be.

We ask your special gifts of grace and inspiration for our married people — for those long-married, or about to be married, or about to give up on marriage. O God, you know the powerful forces of today that work against a happy and satisfying marriage. Give us insight and wisdom to understand our problems and grant us the resolution and strength to solve them.

We pray for the wife in conflicting roles of career and marriage and family; for the husband struggling with social change which challenges male customs; for the divorced person still angry perhaps, hurt over feeling rejected, or embittered by love gone sour or even violent; for the widow or widower feeling as though half of the self has been torn away and overwhelmed with surprising tides of grief; for those single persons seeking that one other person who could complete the longing for genuine love and productive partnership. For these we pray, O God, and for all hurting souls in bruised relationships. Speak to each of us in our deepest need, loving Father, and infuse us with your gracious Spirit, that we might move forward to the better self, the better love, and the better day you have planned for us.

Through Jesus Christ our Lord. Amen.

Discussion Questions

1. Some married people seem to have a need to "take control" of the partner or "to possess" the partner so that the partner feels used, thwarted, and repressed. Is this urge to control and possess a form of greed? How would you describe it? Do some partners want to be "possessed" and "controlled"? How would you describe a healthy relationship?

2. Is anger better expressed or left unexpressed? Some people believe it is unchristian to be angry and to express anger. How do you feel? Can expressed anger have a positive outcome? What suggestions would you have for the expression of anger between partners?

3. Everyone wants to talk; no one wants to listen. It's hard to find a good listener today, even in the marriage partner, perhaps especially in the marriage partner. What steps might partners take to improve communication? Are there things partners should not communicate? What should be high on the list of priorities for good communication?

Chapter 14

How To Stay In Love

*Be subject to one another out
of reverence for Christ.
Wives, be subject to your
husbands, as to the Lord.
Husbands, love your wives, as
Christ loved the church and
gave himself up for her.*
— Ephesians 5:21-22, 25

"Well, it's finally over," he said to me, breathing a sigh of relief with a touch of wistfulness in his voice. "After two long years, the divorce is final. We signed all the papers just the other day."

"You must be glad to be finished with that ordeal," I commented. "It can be a draining experience." "It really can," he said. "It's sad in a way, to bring a marriage to a close, to break off something we thought would last until, as the ceremony says, 'death do us part.' You have all the shared experiences, of course, the kids and grandkids, the common memories, and all that. There's a certain sadness about sort of closing the door on all that."

Then he went on: "Yet it had to be. It had been a miserable marriage for at least fifteen years. We had made love only two or three times in all those years. And when I think back on it, I knew almost from the beginning the marriage was a mistake. Yet we stuck it out for over forty years. But as I look back on it, it was for the most part, a miserable forty years. I would never do it again."

Contrast them with another couple I knew. After burying the sister-in-law of this woman, we went back to the house for refreshments. The woman said to me, "You know, my husband and I have been married for almost fifty years, and I am happier now by far than on my wedding day. My husband has been the best thing that ever happened to me." She continued, "It is as if I found my other self in him and he in me. We complete each other and draw each other out into a better self than we could ever be by ourselves. I don't know what I'll do if he precedes me in death."

She was not Pollyannaish. There had been difficult times in their marriage. Yet the difficult times had served to increase their love and companionship rather than decrease them. It is safe to say those factors were at work in my in-laws' marriage, who celebrated their sixtieth wedding anniversary. And my parents would have celebrated their sixtieth wedding anniversary if my father had lived a year longer.

However, marriages of that duration are more and more difficult to find. Sometimes, divorce seems the only answer to a bad marriage. But be it first, second, or third marriage, we wonder, will it last? Will it be a lifelong companionship of deepening love? How does one stay in love today?

I.

Note first the importance of *communication*. Most marriages in trouble suffer from a breakdown of communication.

The charming story of Adam and Eve in the Garden of Eden is disarming in its simplicity and profundity. Unlike the first creation story where male and female are created primarily for procreation, in the second creation story, located in the Garden of Eden, they are created primarily for companionship and communication. In this story, Adam is created first. But since he is lonely, God creates the animal kingdom to be with Adam, but he is still lonely.

Not to be defeated in his grand design of love, God causes a deep sleep to come over Adam, and then from Adam's rib fashions a lovely, curvaceous Eve. It is said that when Adam awoke and saw Eve standing before him in the "altogether," he stood and sang the entire "Hallelujah Chorus" without taking a breath! It was plain to see that God had taken a big step toward solving the problem of loneliness, not to mention desire. "This at last is bone of my bone, and flesh of my flesh." "Hallelujah!"

The creation story says Eve was created to be Adam's helpmate, someone to be alongside him as an equal partner in promulgating the human species and in having dominion over the earth. But the Hebrew word for helpmate also implies "answerer," one who has the capacity to answer back in human language and feelings. The animals may well be named by Adam and may have the capacity to respond to his command and be trained by him, but despite all the tail-wagging, a dog is still not man's best friend! It was Eve who knew human language and touch and feelings and could respond in kind. "Hallelujah!"

Man and woman were created for one another, to be together in sociability, to share deeply human feelings, to communicate, to be known and accepted and understood. It is as if God was seeking to express himself in the powerful attraction of masculinity and femininity. Through the articulation of maleness and femaleness God himself comes more and more to self-actualization and self-fulfillment. Thus good communication has about it an ecstatic, almost divine, dimension. Not only are men and women fulfilled; it is as if creation itself is, in some small way, coming into fulfillment when we are truly heard and understood and loved, as well as when we feel we have truly articulated our deepest feelings.

Many couples have lost the companionship of good communication because they no longer really listen. Consequently, we need to bite our tongues, open ourselves to our mates, and receive the feelings and insights they long to share. We need to ask questions to draw the other out. We need to seek out how the other feels without being so quick to let him or her know how we feel in judgment or criticism.

Many couples and friends have fallen into bad manners which need to be corrected. For example, the root meaning of companionship is "to share bread with another." Regrettably, many couples and families eat together less and less, or eat on the run. Others have their nose in a newspaper or magazine or have the television blaring during dinner. Good eating habits and civilized table manners can go a long way toward good communication. Good communication can be a powerful tool for staying in love.

II.

How do we stay in love? *We have to compromise.*

Consider this scene. It is night in Madison Square Garden in New York City. The place is packed and the crowd has been warm and enthusiastic. "Ol' Blue Eyes" himself, Frankie the Crooner, is holding forth in later years as Frank Sinatra ("Chairman of the Board"), now an accepted American institution something like Bob Hope or Jack Benny.

As usual, his orchestra is lush and scintillating, aglow with rhythm and expression. The audience has felt affirmed and entertained, inspired and reassured that in an age of change, Frank can still belt it out in familiar ways that touch the soul.

A hush comes over the crowd, the spotlight comes up for the last number and in the lush, uniquely warm human tones we know so well, he begins to sing about how as he faces the final curtain he has done it "my way."

With the audience enthralled, he continues to sing of regrets he overcame, of times he bit off more than he could chew, managing to eat it up and spit it out anyway. He sings of laughter and tears and losing, and doing it his way nevertheless.

I like that song — especially the way he sings it and the orchestra plays it. There is a lot of truth in it — truth having to do with being something other than a doormat, truth having to do with taking charge of our lives, of meeting challenges and being responsible, truth of being courageous and forthright rather than wimpish and whimpering. Let the record show we took the blows, and did it our way.

Nonetheless, carried to the extremes, the song is really antithetical to basic Christian teachings — teachings of courtesy, kindness, thoughtfulness, of love which does not insist on its own way; teachings having to do with looking to the needs of others, teachings having to do with service and even with sacrifice. The question is, what is the proper way in Christian marriage, my way or yours?

At first glance it looks as though Christian scripture would have wives do it their husband's way. Here are the familiar words again: "Wives, be subject to your husbands, as to the Lord. For the husband

154

is the head of the wife as Christ is the head of the church, his body, and is himself its savior."

For centuries, this scripture was read at weddings, but it is difficult to get it read at weddings anymore. Brides won't allow it. And it is difficult to get it read in my home.

I like another passage in Peter's First Letter which suggests wives should be subject to their husbands as Sarah was subject to her husband and called him Lord. Although my name is not Abraham, my wife's name is Sara.

But she ignores that passage too. I tell Sara she is developing a Thomas Jefferson Bible. When Jefferson came to a passage in the Bible he thought irrelevant or didn't like, he ripped it out. He ended up with a rather thin Bible!

In the social context of the time, Paul did espouse the equality of men and women, for all are one in Christ, even slave and master, Jew and Gentile. Yet just as Paul, in the context of the times, did not advocate the overthrow of slavery, neither did he attempt to overthrow the patriarchal structure. There was to be authority in church, society, and home; and as Christ was head of the church to prevent selfish anarchy, so was the husband head of the family to preserve order.

But, as Bob Dylan used to sing, "The times, they are a changin'." Francine Klagsbrun tells of a highly successful plastic surgeon in New York whose wife went back to work not because they needed the money, but because she needed the freedom and self-worth and independence a separate job and income could give her. Her husband had never told her how much he made, nor had he included her in financial decisions.

"He controls the money so he makes the decisions about how we spend it. If I were earning what he is earning and he were earning what I am earning, our lives would be completely different. I would have the power to make the decisions about how we use our money." Lila continued about how good it was to have her own money. "I don't feel so powerless anymore" (*Married People*, Francine Klagsbrun, pp. 40, 41).

Uneasy about being an adjunct to a husband's life and uncomfortable with always having to live vicariously through the successes and failures of husbands and children, it is no wonder women want to get out on their own, to establish their self-worth in the broader marketplace, to build self-esteem in independent success and to gain power through financial resources of their own. They want equal pay for equal work, which no longer assumes the man as the breadwinner. They want to be able to get credit in their own names, not just their husbands'. With their talents and abilities too long sublimated and repressed, they want to come into their own as full human beings.

It is no wonder men are a little confused, frustrated, and even angered. They are confused about what women want. They have suffered upsets and inconveniences. They wonder whatever happened to the unspoken, traditional understanding of the roles of husband and wife. They no longer seem to be at the center of the marriage and family. They still bring home the bacon but seem to get little credit for it.

Besides, even when they take up jobs their wives used to do, they are not sure they want them doing them. For example, Jason, a New York plastic surgeon, made the arrangements for his daughter's sweet sixteen party at one of the more expensive hotels. His wife complained about the expense, but what she was sore about, says Klagsbrun, was losing her power in her customary areas — areas such as the social calendar and children's events and family celebrations.

Emotional power has to do with the balance or imbalance of dependencies within a marriage. It has to do with the psychic need one partner has for another, or the power that neediness gives the other, says Klagsbrun (*ibid.*, p. 58). Today, perhaps as never before in the war between the sexes, there is a struggle as to who will "wear the pants" in the family. (You'll notice there never is a struggle as to who will wear the dress in the family. Husbands in dresses and high heels always raise eyebrows, whereas women in suits and ties do not!)

Who does call the shots in a marriage? Whose tastes and values prevail? Who decides how children will be disciplined, how holidays will be spent, how the household will be organized, and what the family rules will be?

If it has traditionally been thought men controlled this sector, we cannot be quite as sure. The emotional power play is more complex, more subtle. For example, my seminary professor of Old Testament and Hebrew was a native of Japan. Japanese society, said the professor, was very patriarchal. Officially, the man was the head of everything. But in actuality, he said, the woman controlled everything. She was the power behind the throne.

So women may appear weak, meek, sweet, dependent, and helpless. But in so appearing they really manipulate others to do their bidding. And men are uncertain. One man of my acquaintance calls all the shots at home, but at work his secretary is in control. To be sure, a life of mutual subjection can be a life of mutual dullness and boredom. But so can a life of constant contention and selfishness.

We can get tired of contentiousness. One husband said, "We got along just great for six years. Then she decided to come back home." On the one hand we are intent on doing our thing and fulfilling ourselves and finding ourselves. And yet we feel the need for connectedness and interrelatedness and someone to care about us, whether we live or die. If we are on the one hand narcissistic and hedonistic, on the other hand we are lonely and alienated.

But Paul really suggests compromise rather than conquest. He recommends mutual subjection rather than exploitation and domination. The word "compromise" means "to promise together," suggesting give and take, courtesy, forbearance, and thoughtfulness. Love, says Paul in his famous love chapter, 1 Corinthians 13, does not insist on its own way.

The truth is that in all of life, in order to get along, we have to make compromises and adjustments. The world does not always bend to our will. We have to learn to get along, to adjust.

So too in our marriages and relationships. Frank Sinatra may be able to do it "my way," but most of us need to learn to do it our way. And if we can communicate and compromise, we can stay in love, for a richer, fuller life.

Prayer

Eternal God, whose power sustains and permeates the universe and whose subtle presence draws us out of preoccupation with ourselves to look upon you and your larger causes for the world, we come to you to be reminded of your greatness and our smallness. Like seedlings in springtime you have made us for growth and development, so in prayer we come for life-giving light and nutrients. Be pleased to feed our souls and minds, O Lord.

It has pleased you, O Lord, in your creative wisdom, to make us male and female, masculine and feminine. All the living world seems to be a ritual dance of mating and reproduction. In our youth we see the powerful forces of eros hard at work, and in ourselves we have known and continue to know the strength of desire and craving for love. Sometimes, we confess, O Lord, that perhaps the ancient fertility cults were right, that eros is the most powerful force of all, and that we are driven by it and subservient to it.

And yet you have called us to the fullness of personhood, to bring into control these wild horse passions within to serve you and ourselves. Grant that we might be disciplined rather than dillettante, expressive rather than repressive, faithful rather than fickle, warm and fully human rather than cold and aloof. Remind us that you created us male and female and that we are not to despise our bodies and our sensual passions, but to cherish them and fulfill them in responsible ways.

We pray especially for couples who in their relationships seek satisfaction of desire and fulfillment of self. If we have been demanding and demeaning, help us relax more into thoughtfulness and understanding. If we have been cold and aloof and defensive, release us from our fears and hang-ups so that we might experience the full joy and ecstasy of human loving. If in smugness we are content with our virtues while critical of our partner's failings, help us to humble ourselves to see more honestly our own annoying idiosyncrasies. If in arrogance we have done all the talking, demanding to be understood, grant us the modesty and strength and patience to listen and to understand.

O God, how earnestly we pray for marriages today. See what enormous pressures couples often endure. Be pleased to aid us, that peace and release and joy and fulfillment might come to us all.

In Christ's name we pray. Amen.

Discussion Questions

1. For many people money is power, even in a marriage. Should the marriage partner who makes the most money wield the most power in the marriage? Should money and power be linked at all in marriage? What advice would you give to couples regarding marriage, money, and power?

2. Some people claim they find their true self in marriage, that they really blossom and become the self they dreamed of becoming. Do you know people like that? How might a person help a partner toward fulfillment and the realization of true selfhood? What would be some of the most common hindrances in achieving that goal?

3. Authority issues are common in marriage. The Judeo-Christian scriptures commonly assume the husband is to be the head of the wife and family and household. Many women today chafe at that advice and some men are uncomfortable with it. Who should be in charge in a marriage and family? How should Christians handle the authority question?

Chapter 15

How To Love Marriage And Family

*Continue in what you have learned
and have firmly believed, knowing from
whom you learned it and how from
childhood you have been acquainted
with the sacred writings which are
able to instruct you for salvation
through faith in Jesus Christ.*
— 2 Timothy 3:14-15

We have been addressing the challenge of how to love. When we spoke about "how to love men," at least the men were in favor of the idea. And when we spoke about "how to love women," the women responded very favorably to the idea. Men and women these days seem ready to take love wherever they can find it.

But how about marriage and family? Is there anyone around who still claims to love marriage and revere family? Is it not popular to sneer at the politically incorrect Dan Quayles who at least attempt to speak up for the family? And are not so-called "family values" scoffed at as hangovers from a naive, sentimental past?

And who bothers to get married any more? Even though statistics show that people who live together before marriage have a higher divorce rate when they do marry, and even though sexual permissiveness and promiscuity are touted in almost every movie and television show we see, and even though commitment is one thing everyone longs for but no one is willing to give, marriage is not held in high esteem among the popular, greed-driven, culture-forming and opinion-making elite.

If in times past there were indeed a number of shotgun weddings hurriedly arranged to legitimize the sooner-than-expected baby, today celebrities, financiers, politicians, and other leaders not only flaunt living together without benefit of clergy, they proudly parade a pregnancy out of wedlock and may or may not eventually announce their marriage.

The public philanderers par excellence, the Kennedy brothers (not to mention their father), titillated the media and the imaginations of millions, and excited the aspirations of Kennedy wannabe's like Gary Hart and apparently Bill Clinton who imitated not only hairstyles and mannerisms, but the philandering too. Who is the would-be celebrity or sports hero or Kennedyesque politician who would want to be known for his devotion to marriage and family? Certainly not Bob Packwood, whose philandering and sexual harassment were exceeded only by a desperate ego that had to record it all in diaries.

Who loves family and marriage and family values? In today's "anything goes" mentality the media and entertainment industry know there's more money to be made on *Indecent Proposal*, *Fatal Attraction*, *Basic Instinct*, and so forth, than any movie or situation comedy or novel which exalts fidelity to spouse, commitment to marriage and children, and devotion to ideals and community over the individual's frantic pursuit of personal happiness.

The families in today's spotlight leave little to be desired. Tonya Harding's family life was tawdry; the Menendez brothers killed their parents because the father allegedly sexually abused the boys. Bill and Hillary seem to have had a rocky past, if not present. Burt Reynolds, painful though it was, he says, got a divorce at last. John and Lorena Bobbitt perhaps should have divorced long before his sexual abuse and her primitive reprisal.

Pick up any newspaper or magazine. Listen to any television report. The statistics are appalling. Twenty-eight percent of American children never finish high school, and of those who do, nearly fifty percent are functionally illiterate. AIDS is spreading rapidly. Sexually transmitted diseases are epidemic.

Physical abuse of children and women is high. Drug abuse abounds. Homelessness, depression, teenage suicides, single mothers in large numbers at or below the poverty level are increasing rapidly.

On and on the sad and startling statistics go. But the church is one place where we can take a stand. And our own personal and family lives are places we can make a difference.

How do we love marriage and family?

I.

For one thing, we shall have to *love family and marriage more than self.*

This may sound strange indeed to a generation that has inscribed Thomas Jefferson's "life, liberty and the pursuit of happiness" in the sinews of their hearts. If ever there were an age insisting on rights more than responsibilities, ours is it. Former Education Secretary William Bennett said that in their study of students' handbooks in educational institutions across the country, the contents were 99 percent about rights and only one percent about responsibilities.

The idealism of the '60s, prompted in part by Kennedy's "ask not what your country can do for you, but ask what you can do for your country," led to the Peace Corps, community service, and reform movements by the dozen. People were devoted to issues and causes bigger than themselves.

But the '80s, the decade of huge money-making and greed, blunted the edge of idealism. With big dollars in our portfolios and bank accounts, we moved quickly to fulfill every hedonistic desire and to achieve every fantasy. In the pursuit of individual happiness, it was full speed ahead, marriage and the family and other entangling commitments be damned.

A few years ago, University of California sociologist Robert Bellah and his colleagues published a book titled *Habits of the Heart*. In it, he chronicled the intense individualism and the personal pursuit of private happiness of many Americans. Not only did they place work and family at the service of their grinning ego-seeking contentment, even God was seen as a kind of personal valet to aid them with problems, or to call in to assist them in achieving power, success, and money. Rather than human beings created in God's image, to reflect his glory, God was created in human image to help them with their own glory.

163

In 1993, Bellah and his colleagues came out with a sequel to *Habits of the Heart*, this one called *The Good Society*. Their thesis is that Americans have continued their restless pursuit of the good life for themselves at almost any cost — especially the cost of supporting the very institutions of community, church, school, and family which make the core of the good life possible.

This is symbolized by a story out of Los Angeles a few years ago during a serious water shortage. Strict water rationing rules were in effect. Guess where they were violated most? In poor neighborhoods, running fire hydrants wide open for a summer shower? In middle class neighborhoods fastidiously clean, believing cleanliness was next to godliness? Oh no, not in these areas. It was in wealthy areas where water usage was excessive. It was as if they were saying, "I've worked hard to get this far to achieve this much to buy this house with all its advanced comforts, and no one is going to deprive me of the comforts and happiness of my long showers and frequent baths." Community good was easily sacrificed for individual selfishness.

Dr. Bellah quotes one researcher who says we are in a "post-nuclear family trend." Instead of the individual belonging to the family, it is the family that belongs to the individual, to be at the service of the individual, to be used by the individual, and then rejected or discarded when it is no longer useful. We have moved from a child-centered family to an adult-centered family. Says Bellah, "in recent decades individual fulfillment has ranked even higher as a central cultural value ..." (*The Good Society,* p. 46).

Even though there are many manifestations of family and definitions of family, the truth still remains that children as well as adults need the bonding support, intimacy, and sense of commitment which come from a strong family. While the state and the economy have encroached on many areas of personal, social, and family life, and while many of us have transferred our primary location of emotional identification and socialization to the workplace, and while for many of us it can be said we only live to work rather than work to live — while all that can be and is being said, the larger truth is that we need to learn to love marriage and family more than self and its insatiable quest for happiness. The "job culture," says Bellah, "has expanded at the expense of family culture."

Besides, in all our pursuit of happiness, are we really happy? With only five percent of the world's population, we consume more than fifty percent of the world's drugs. We spend $460 billion a year on entertainment, which is, for the most part, escapist and diversionary rather than challenging.

So many of our institutions have become dysfunctional. We are very cynical about our political system, and rightly so. We distrust a lot of business and professional people whom we see as devoted only to self and greed. We neglect adequate attention to our communities, so our local village sues the only two churches serving within its boundaries. Why would the citizens of the village allow such a thing? Schools suffer from both parental attack and inattention. Churches themselves become tiresome battlegrounds of trivial and sometimes lethal politics. Doesn't it surprise you how much hatred church people can generate for ministers and other church leaders?

We need then, say Bellah and others, a renewed commitment to marriage and family, a commitment that is both higher and deeper than our commitment to our ephemeral personal happiness. The responsibility of spouse and children is a higher claim than the responsibility to personal happiness — whatever that might be.

The surprising thing is that when we exercise this commitment to those closest to us, we discover the ancient truth of Jesus' words, "He who saves his life, loses it; he who loses his life for my sake and the gospel's, finds it."

II.

How do we love marriage and family? *We love them by placing love of God above all else.*

Did you read the alarming news? The alarming news about American children being gunned down in homes, streets, and schools? The Children's Defense Fund announced that gun violence kills one child every two hours or "one classroomful every two days." Murder, they say in their 1994 *State of America's Children* report, is the third leading cause of death among children ages five to fourteen, following accidents and cancer.

165

Did you read about it? Two boys are being held for the rape of an eleven-year-old girl. And how old are the boys? They were thirteen at the time. Did you see it on *60 Minutes*? The interviews with the juvenile murderers? Did they have remorse over their heinous crime? Not most of them. Police officials tell us that increasingly young murderers, rapists, and other perpetrators of brutal crime have little or no remorse when they are caught. It is not a question of moral or immoral. They are amoral, without any sense of morality or conscience.

Did you read it? The F.B.I. is putting an additional ten agents on the streets of Washington, D.C., to investigate crimes. F.B.I. Director Louis Freeh said, "Crime is so severe in Washington that extraordinary steps must be taken." On and on it goes, our papers and magazines and news programs are full of stories of crime, drug abuse, sex abuse, immorality, and amorality. Do you not wonder if our society is dying and decaying at its very core? I do.

That is why we need to love our marriages and families by teaching ourselves and our children to love God more than self and pleasure and success. How do we do that? We do it the same way as his grandmother Lois and his mother Eunice did it for Timothy, Saint Paul's young associate. They taught him the sacred scriptures from childhood on up through his youth. They inculcated spiritual and moral values from day one so that Timothy grew up to be a stalwart Christian leader and exemplar of the true spiritual life.

And where do we learn the sacred scriptures? In church, for one place. Thank God we have many adults who are committed to stamping out biblical illiteracy and ethical amorality. But it's an uphill battle as we all contend with the allurements and vices and seductions of the present age, especially if they promise money or pleasure.

But our children need to be in church. Where will they learn spiritual values if not in church and Sunday School and family? Where will they develop an inward sense of right and wrong, the consciousness of a law higher than their own feelings and lusts, a sense of accountability to something higher than the driving force of their hormones and their need for ego gratification and a desperate sense of belonging?

Paul told Timothy that the holy Scriptures are profitable to teach young people how to grow up to be spiritually mature. We parents are rightly concerned that our children excel academically, athletically, and socially. But how many of us exercise as much concern for their love of God and Jesus and their devotion to spiritual graciousness and a sense of service above self?

Paul says the scriptures are valuable for reproof and correction. Think of it, an eternal source of truth outside the self and its whims, reproving us, showing us where we are wrong and where we can use improvement. What teenager has ever admitted he or she was wrong? What adult today actually confesses to his or her spouse, "I'm sorry, dear. I was wrong. Will you please forgive me?"

We all need an authority higher than the self, higher than social convention and cultural custom, by which to direct our lives. We all need a "north star" for spiritual and moral navigation in an age adrift in the fogs of whims and fads and fancies and relativisms.

Paul says that if we teach the scripture regularly, if we lift up our eyes to God more than self, if we devote ourselves to the one who created us and re-created us in love, then we will be well-trained for righteousness in place of wickedness. We will be complete, mature, and better equipped to withstand the onslaught of greed and violence and self-love and amorality so powerful in today's culture.

How do we love marriage and family? By loving it more than our selfish pursuit of happiness, which is fueled largely by our affluence. Ask yourself, where would you be, who would you be, if you were deprived of your present job or money? Who would be there to love you and support you and stand by you? It will be the family if you have not sacrificed them to your selfish pursuit of private happiness.

How do we love marriage and family? By putting the love of God highest of all through teaching the sacred scriptures. Just who is shaping the lives of our young? If it is not parents and teachers and ministers, it will be, and often is, the peer group, and the powerful youth culture of MTV, music, magazines, movies, and fashions, all of which are fueled by money and often by greed.

Paul says to Timothy that the last days will be full of stress, when people will be lovers of self, lovers of money, ungrateful, disobedient to parents, inhuman, amoral, slanderers, treacherous, arrogant, conceited, having a form of religion, but denying its renewing, transforming power.

Are these the last days? Sometimes it feels like it, does it not? And when these negative values prevail, we are always closer to the end of the age. In their place it is time to renew our commitment to love of men, women, marriage, and family.

Prayer

Almighty God, creator of all the galaxies and universes, who fashioned the worlds through the aeons of geologic time which are but days to you and ages to us; and who, in the far reaches of your mind and power, brought the living cell into being, shaping and molding it in millions of ways to give us the dazzling multiplicity of all living things, it is with awe and reverence we bow the knee and raise our voices to adore you. How wondrously and marvelously have all things been made.

It has pleased you to make us male and female. In your divine wisdom you have provided chromosomes both x and y, making us so different, yet so alike; bringing forth a panoply of human variety, yet giving us the capacity to communicate and to understand one another. Distinct and different, you have designed us for a symphony of humanity, to make divine music in harmonious and satisfying relationships.

And yet we must confess our discordant living and playing. Strife and disharmony characterize too much of our relating. Hatred and violence have broken out with new force, not only in the family of nations, but also in our families close at hand. O God, forgive these terrible infractions of your divine plan, and bring us again to the harmonies you intend.

Look this day with special favor upon our families so in need of guidance, wisdom, and empowerment from above. See how powerful are the forces which tear us apart, which wreak havoc with our communication and understanding, which rip apart the carefully woven tapestries of love and destroy the precarious intimacies and trust built on such fragile foundations.

How earnestly we beseech your help for mothers and fathers to focus on the basic and essential eternal truths for family living. How desperately we pray for children to be weaned from selfishness and violence, from a sense of insignificance and feeling of indifference and rejection. Grant us the strong help we need as a church and society to take control of our family life, to wrest it from the hands of the greedy, the destructive, the foolish, the licentious, the resentful, the hateful, and all other enemies of true love and healthy relationships. Be pleased to grant us your much needed blessing, O God.

In Christ's name we pray. Amen.

Discussion Questions

1. Many observers claim that today the family takes a back seat to individual fulfillment. The home and family, say some, are a stopping-off point for rest and refueling. The emotional center for many is no longer the family, but the workplace or school or peer group. How do you feel about these observations? Has family life improved or declined in the last thirty or forty years? What suggestions would you have for improved family life?

2. Sports, academic achievement, and peer approval seem to be much more important to families today than church or spiritual principles or family values. In some communities, Christian churches either support or condone sports or other community activities on Sunday mornings. Should Christians object or just have services on another day and time? How might Christians instill more permanent values for family living?

3. "The family that prays together stays together," says the old platitude. Do many families today actually pray together or even eat together? What steps might be taken to improve family spirituality?

Chapter 16

How To Help The Family

Put on ... compassion, kindness,
lowliness, meekness, and patience,
forbearing one another and, if one
has a complaint against another,
forgiving each other; as the Lord
has forgiven you, so you also must
forgive. And above all these put
on love, which binds everything
together in perfect harmony.

— Colossians 3:12-14

It is a truism to say that many of our families today are in trouble and under a great deal of stress. Our divorce rate is the highest in the world. Over sixty percent of children now born will spend part of their lives in a single-parent family, most of which will be headed by females who are struggling not only emotionally, but financially.

Over twenty percent of our children are born out of wedlock, and we continue to have over a million abortions a year, mostly for birth control purposes. Persons living alone account for about twenty-five percent of our households. Over one-half of the mothers with preschool children are now in the workforce. Says Peter Morrison of Rand Corporation's Population Research Center, "Fewer and fewer American families conform to traditional stereotypes. People think they are seeing departures from the norm," says Morrison, "but departures are now 75 percent of the norm."

People today marry later — often in their late twenties or early thirties — and divorce more quickly than ever before. More than two million unmarried couples are living together — four times as many as in 1970. Indeed, one woman of the middle generation commenting on this fact said, rather sheepishly, that she and her husband were virgins when they married.

But today it is different. Two college kids were having a slight argument about their relationship. "I don't mind your mother living with us," the fellow was saying, "but I do wish she'd wait until we get married."

One sociologist says that a teen pregnancy study shows that forty percent of today's fourteen-year-old girls will be pregnant at least once by the age of twenty. Sexual looseness is filtering down into the junior high schools. Young people seem to be looking for love, or at least sexual expression, at alarmingly young ages. And any parent who has had to cope with a pregnant or sexually diseased child may well wonder what is happening to our culture.

One sociologist writes: "In a country supposedly bent on the pursuit of excellence, it's ironic that we often settle for 'fair' — even 'poor' — when it comes to family." He says if half of our businesses or schools failed, we'd be in a panic. But when half of all first marriages end in divorce and when an even higher percentage of second marriages end in divorce, we accept it, he says, as some sort of stopover in the pursuit of happiness and fulfillment.

So we've come into these sacred precincts to help the family — help that can come out of the sacred scriptures. And I would like to suggest three "T's" that can help us — Time, Tenderness, and Theology.

I.

Consider first the matter of *Time*.

In his letter to the Ephesians Paul the Apostle advises us to "redeem the time because the days are evil." Make the most of the time we have, he advises, because there is a lot of evil that can destroy us and our families.

One of the strange benefits of my work as a minister is that I am often in hospitals, nursing homes, and cemeteries. It may surprise you that I might call visits to such unpleasant places "benefits." Nevertheless, as I walk up and down the corridors of hospitals and nursing homes I am reminded to count my blessings for good health and to be thankful for what I *do* have rather than to complain about what I do *not* have.

And cemeteries serve to remind me of the brevity of life — cemeteries I have visited to bury my father, father-in-law, and mother. It seems only yesterday I was a child and youth at my mother's table enjoying her excellent food which was like a sacrament of love. We need to make the most of the time we have.

Families need to spend time together, but studies show that they do not. One study shows that the average five-year-old spends 25 *minutes* a week in close interaction with his father and 25 *hours* a week in close interaction with the television set. It is no wonder then that in a recent survey of kindergartners Dad finished second to the boob tube. Another father, making six figures a year, drives a $70,000 Porsche, but doesn't know the name of the high school his son attends.

Many families, in an effort to spend time together, take an extended automobile trip. We did our share of those with our six children. Erma Bombeck said she and her husband did it with their three. And just before they left they would read a book, written by a woman who has no children, on the joys of traveling with children.

One writer advised putting pillows, snacks, a change of clothes, and some favorite toys in the car where they can be easily reached. Rest stops with walks should be planned every two hours. When you are back on the road, talk about what you saw at the rest stop, although this writer — without child — doesn't say what to do if your ten-year-old son starts to recite loudly in front of all the others the bathroom graffiti. The writer does suggest singing and guessing games. Then Erma Bombeck adds with her characteristic sarcasm and wit, "Well, if that doesn't make you want to go right out and rent a child for your next trip ... nothing will" (*Family: The Ties That Bind — And Gag!*, p. 60).

True, in all our family vacations my wife never quite understood why it was necessary to pack the car the night before and then leave at 5:30 A.M. She would have preferred to see the countryside by daylight rather than by headlight. And when she did see the countryside she thought we probably could have done with less if I had been willing to stop and ask for directions.

But on the other hand, I never quite understood why she could not remember to turn off the iron until we were twenty miles down the freeway, or why it was that our daughter could never remember to take the pet gerbil to her friends before we got across the toll bridge. Nor could I quite understand why at least one of our five daughters had to go to the restroom only thirty minutes after our last stop.

Despite all that, looking back, we have cherished those all-too-rare family times together — those times when I would leave the motel early in the morning to seek out the local bakery for some delicious sweets to enjoy with our fruit and cereal in our room, those times in the summer afternoon tossing squealing children into the air in the motel swimming pool, those times watching the first dives of our daughters and the crashing cannonball of our son, those times relaxing in the afternoon sun or reading the nighttime story with three or four on my lap, or those times of sweet and tender nighttime prayers, or times of tears and comfort — those rich, rare times of love and human bonding.

They were quality times to be sure, and they often took place in the midst of quantity time. Those who argue that they spend quality but not necessarily quantity time with their children may be stretching it a bit. Most of the so-called quality times that we planned for often didn't happen except in the context of quantity time — time when we were just together and surprised by joy in the bonding, the sharing, the love and understanding. Families need time together.

II.

If families need time together, they also need *Tenderness*. As Paul puts it in our text, we are to do away with malice and wrath. We are to be forbearing and forgiving. In a parallel passage in Ephesians he writes, "Be kind to one another, tenderhearted, forgiving one another, as God in Christ forgave you" (Ephesians 4:32).

In this stress-filled, anti-family age parents need to be tender not only with their children, but with each other. After all, child-rearing is an anxiety-producing process. Sociologist Henry Holstege says that "the evidence indicates that married couples are happiest prior to having children, unhappiest during child-rearing years, then happier again when the last child leaves home." Holstege says "Couples with no children indicate a higher degree of marital satisfaction than couples with children" (*The Christian Family*, p. 21). No empty nest syndrome here. I am reminded of Mrs. Smith leading a half-dozen children, getting them on the bus. As she headed toward the back, another passenger, a pleasant elderly man, asked, "Are those your children, or is it some kind of picnic?" Mrs. Smith answered, "They're mine, and it's no picnic!"

Further, says Holstege, there is a romantic complex about parenthood and children. In a movie, the singer is singing "Count Your Blessings" as he tucks his little one in for the night, in a beautiful room all aglow with the radiance of paradise, while the little one lies there angelic in repose — a designer scene of designer children designed by the same childless writer giving advice on how to travel with designer children.

But what the designer romantics and sentimentalists do not show is the child crying all night from colic. Nor does it show the dirty, stinky diapers, the vomit on the pillow, or the retarded or handicapped child. As one author laconically observed, "There is bedwetting all over the world."

Further, says author Michael Novak, "Trying to act fairly to children, each of whom is temperamentally different from myself and from each other, each of whom is at a different stage of perception, is far more baffling than anything Harvard prepared for me" (*ibid.*, p. 21). Then says Henry Holstege, "Some parents reach a point of frustration where they would like to write their sixteen-year-old a note saying, 'find other parents; we resign from being your dad and mother' "(*ibid.*, p. 23).

Parenting is not that easy. Sociologist Philip Slater writes that many Spock-oriented mothers "believe deep in their hearts, that if they did their job well enough all of their children would be creative, intelligent, kind, generous, happy, brave, spontaneous, and good — each, of course, in his or her own special way" (*The Pursuit of Loneliness*, p. 64). Some parents have believed they had to raise the genius, the masterpiece, the super-child and thus became involved in overprogramming their child toward some distant goal.

Consequently, the pressure on children to super-achieve can become unbearable, because the parents' own anxiety and ego are involved. While none of us wishes failure for our children, and while all of us want them to succeed, it may be that we become too harsh and demanding in insisting they live up to our higher and higher expectations.

I remember when I resolved in my own mind not to make the mistakes I perceived my parents had made in raising me. Then one day it dawned on me that I was not only repeating some of their mistakes, but creating some new ones of my own.

Parenting and family living are not always easy. Therefore we need some tenderness in the family, some forgiving and hugging and easing up and some laughter at our foibles. Moms and dads, be tender with each other and with your children. And children, be tender with your parents, especially the ones you have between your sixteenth and twenty-first birthdays and especially the aged ones.

III.

But if the family can be helped by more time and tenderness, it can also be helped by some good *Theology*. To say it another way, the family needs to be centered on a higher authority than itself. It needs to be centered on God.

University of Chicago sociologist Gibson Winter tells the story of some Japanese businessmen visiting in an American home. Following Japanese custom, they addressed their conversation to the father, presuming him to be the head of the house. Sensing that was not working, they began to address their comments to the mother. Further frustrated, they then spoke to the children and discovered that everything fell into place. The children, they discovered, were the real authority of the family, around whom everything revolved.

But if families are confused about authority on the social level, they often are even more confused about authority on the level of ethics, morals, values, and faith. Everyone acknowledges that it is important to have faith, but the question is, "faith in what?"

One young couple, returning to church with their young child in tow, said that was the question which dawned on them. They had grown up in the sixties, and like most young people had started to fade away from the church in their teens. True to form, the college experience took them ever further away from the church. They got married, in the style of the times, barefoot on the beach. In fact, I married them with the sound of the surf in the background.

They made a brief appearance later at the church when they decided to have their baby boy baptized. But now they were back, toddler in hand, ready for the church school experience. "It dawned on us," they told me, "that our son needed to have the same spiritual faith and values instilled in him that we had instilled in us. And it became apparent to us we couldn't do it on our own."

A few years ago, Harvard sociologist David Riesman wrote in his book, *The Lonely Crowd*, that increasingly our society was drifting away from an inner-directed mode to an other-directed mode. Whereas once we had firm religious and spiritual values deeply instilled, we now were subject more to authorities outside ourselves — authorities like opinion polls, columnists, trends, and fashions. If once we had an internal gyroscope of faith and morals which kept us balanced and on course in turbulent times, now we tend to be blown about by the latest "in" thing to do or to believe.

Some parents have unusual notions when it comes to religion and values. Often parents will say that they will not bring their children to church. They want them to make up their own minds about religion when they are old enough. But are they not saying that religion is not important enough for them to teach their children? Would they allow their children to avoid good hygiene or good eating habits or study habits? Would they allow them to make up their own minds on matters of health or behavior or education? We parents try to instill in our children those things we believe to be important.

Oliver Wendell Holmes once wrote that "the first step toward a truer faith is the recognition that I, at any rate, am *not* God." Without God at the center of our families, someone else or something else will take his place. Or as G.K. Chesterton put it so well: "When we stop believing in God, we do not then believe in nothing; we believe in anything."

We fathers and mothers are indeed authorities for our children, and it may be that for some, the children are the authority. But the only adequate authority for all is God — God who helps us keep the balance, who acts like the sun to hold the "solar system" of our family together. So let's pray together — at least at mealtime. And let's go to church, maybe even to family camp, and who knows, even read the Bible together and discuss the divine message for our time.

Is there help for the family? There is indeed. We can help it with more time, tenderness, and good theology.

Prayer

Eternal God of the universe, who as with Moses of old, grants us only a glimpse of your glory, but who in the person of Jesus Christ has made yourself known as loving Father of all who call upon your name, we turn to you in worship as springtime life turns toward the sun. We are conscious of your power beyond our power, your infinite mystery beyond our knowledge forever partial, your infinite imagination and creativity beyond our limited vision and dullness of mind and heart. Praise be to you, O Lord, for creating us to be participants in the great adventure of learning and loving. You are the source and life of all we are, without whom we are as nothing.

Loving Father, who through your Son, Jesus Christ, has entered into the anger and hostility and fallenness of our humanity, draw near to us as we beseech your guidance in our troubled times. If Jesus has come to make us anew, to begin a new humankind to experience the joy and grace and love lost by the old humankind in Adam and Eve, we only can confess our repeated failures in idealizing his new realities. Even now in the more intimate of human relations we often are hostile, defensive, self-righteous, grudge-bearing, and unforgiving. The dreams of the years have disfigured themselves into nightmares. The hopes have inverted themselves into despair. The love which once we knew has been denigrated into a contest of wills and stubborn resolution.

Loving Father, who looks into the depths of human hearts and knows us better than we know ourselves, have pity upon us and forgive these repeated failures of love. If perfect love casts out fear, help us again to be renewed in the knowledge of your love and to be encouraged to reach out in love toward one another.

And for our special needs we are bold to pray, believing you hear us and grant our petitions according to your will. We pray for families broken by death or divorce, that insight and strength might be theirs for a new day. We pray for those alone without nearby assurance of a loved one, that new friends will be found in whom your loving presence is manifested. We pray for children with difficulty in home or school, that resolution of their problems might occur so that they might grow into a new and healthy self-concept. And for parents exhausted and weary in the well-doing of child-rearing, we ask a new vision of their potential and new vitality for love and nurturing.

Through Jesus Christ our Lord. Amen.

Discussion Questions

1. Critics say many families spend very little time together so as to build a family unit and identity. What kinds of things might contemporary families do to improve identity and intimacy? What kinds of things should they avoid doing?

2. Some suggest that for married couples, the child-rearing years are the unhappiest rather than the happiest. Would you agree or disagree? Why? Is the "empty nest" syndrome a fiction? What do you think? How should couples prepare for the "empty nest"?

3. Some parents believe children should be allowed to make up their own minds when it comes to religion. Should parents strive to instill firm religious beliefs and values in their children or should they remain neutral and allow children to decide for themselves? Why? Why not?

Chapter 17

The Family As More Than Accessory

*For the grace of God has appeared
for the salvation of all men, training
us to renounce irreligion and worldly
passions, and to live sober, upright,
and godly lives in this world.*

— Titus 2:11-12

Are you as concerned about the family as I am? Many people are.

In a special issue on the future, *U.S. News and World Report* predicted that "tomorrow's children will grow up with several sets of parents and an assortment of half-and-step-siblings." As a matter of fact, their predictions about tomorrow are rapidly becoming true in today's world. If the rate of divorce and remarriage continues, in just three years, step-families will outnumber biological, first-marriage families.

Consider some more startling facts about marriage and family. Over sixty percent of the children born last year will spend part of their lives in a single-parent family, most of which are headed by females. Twenty percent of the children born in 1985 were born out of wedlock. Persons living alone account for 25 percent of households. And over one half of the mothers with preschool children are now in the work force.

Consider these startling statistics from the Children's Defense Fund as to what happens in one day of American life. In one day in American life five teenagers commit suicide, 7,742 teenagers become sexually active, 609 teenagers get syphilis or gonorrhea, 988 children are abused, 3,288 children run away from home, and 2,269 children are born out of wedlock. All that in one day of American life.

Peter Morrison of Rand Corporation's Population Research Center says, "Fewer and fewer American families conform to traditional stereotypes ... People think they are seeing departures from the norm, but departures are now 75 percent of the norm" (*Wall Street Journal*, 9-25-86, p. 1). People marry later, have fewer children and divorce more quickly than ever before. More than two million unmarried couples are living together — four times as many as in 1970.

Robert S. Welch has written that "a teen pregnancy rate shows that forty percent of today's fourteen year-old girls will be pregnant at least once by the age of 20" (*Focus On The Family*, January 1987). Apparently the pill and other contraception devices are not working. Sexual experience among teenagers is becoming more and more prevalent so that by college age virgins are not only the minority but the ridiculed minority. A little boy asked his father, "Daddy, what's a virgin?" The father replied, "It's a kind of forest!" Many of our college students have turned their dorms into little more than brothels without pay. In an academically elite Eastern college it is customary for many girls to sleep with a different boy every weekend. Promiscuity seems to be at an all-time high among some of our most talented youth. Personal morals and ethics seem to be a joke.

But from the biblical perspective and from the Christian point of view, the disintegration of families and morals is no laughing matter. Personal morals and ethics seem to be peripheral and irrelevant for many; and for others the family is seen only as an accessory to modern life — and a troublesome accessory at that.

I.

We are to be reminded that our Christian faith affirms the family as a primary unit of society. But today it has come to be regarded as an accessory to the economy.

Sociologists have made numerous observations about the tremendous transitions from the agricultural to the industrial age. To a considerable extent the transition from agrarian to industrial has been made within the memory of many. Most Americans are only two or three generations removed from the farm and agrarian society. If not in our own experience, then in the experience of family stories we remember the connectedness of rural and small town America — where family units were primary. Sundays were times for gathering with grandparents, uncles and aunts, and cousins.

In an agrarian economy, children were an economic asset. Farmers hoped especially for boys to help them with the farm work and mothers hoped for girls who could help them with the housework and food preparation and preservation. Even in small towns or the ethnic neighborhoods of larger cities, children were often an economic asset where they helped in the family business, be it a service station, grocery, or drug store.

But in an industrial, urbanized society, not only was the family fragmented in work location, it was also buffeted by new economic pressures. Children became a distinct economic liability costing thousands upon thousands of dollars, not only in birth, but in child-rearing and education. Rather than alleviating family economic pressures, children added to them. And if medical and college costs continue to rise, the pressure will become even more intense.

Children's rising expectations also add to the economic pressure. One man said, "My kids don't think they're having a good time unless they're doing something we can't afford."

Perhaps this is one reason why families are getting smaller and why couples are waiting until later to have children. Perhaps it also helps explain why childless couples seem to report a happier married life, as family sociologist Henry Holstege has asserted.

One of the biggest phenomena to occur lately has been the entry of women into the work force. For single women in a strong career orbit, marriage and family become less and less attractive as well as less and less possible. The unmarried, attractive career women over thirty is a growing phenomenon. It is this woman who, says *Psychology Today* magazine, often becomes the "other woman" in today's affairs.

But married women have also entered the work force in great numbers. As noted earlier, one half of mothers of preschool children have gone to work outside the home. In order to maintain the expected standard of living two incomes are needed in place of one. In addition to that, many women do not find marriage and family emotionally satisfying, so they look for significance and meaning outside the traditional patterns of motherhood, marriage, and management.

Besides, the demands of children can make parenting frustrating. Children have it made today, says Joey Adams. Their mothers drive them everywhere — to school, to the movies, to dancing lessons, to baseball and hockey, to their friends' homes. I know one boy who wanted to run away from home and his mother said, "Wait, I'll drive you!" Another mother reversed it, saying it was her children who drove her back to work!

But the nagging emotional questions won't go away. Our social and family problems seem to increase rather than decrease. We suffer from a deep emotional emptiness, a pervasive loneliness and meaninglessness we try to fill with drugs and excessive alcohol. We claim that what is important with children is "quality time" rather than quantity time. But that can be a rather specious argument.

Is the family only an accessory to our economic needs and success drives? It seems so with many. But very few people on their deathbeds have ever said, "I wish I'd spent more time at the office."

II.

If our faith affirms the primacy of the family, it also affirms the primacy of concern for others over blatant concern for self. Love for others is at the heart of our faith, and that surely means family first of all.

No doubt, the biblical injunctions to deny oneself, take up a cross and follow Jesus, seem quaint to many, super-religious to others. In an age devoted to hedonism and in a time when narcissism seems only natural, devotion to a higher good seems far too demanding. In the 1960s and 1970s there was a greatly increased emphasis on self-fulfillment and self-expression. "We encourage people to do their thing," says Frank Furstenberg, University of Pennsylvania sociologist. "They begin to feel it's not only their right but their obligation" (*Wall Street Journal, op. cit.*).

In the Pauline letter to Titus we have a list of virtues to be practiced by Christian men and women, both older and younger. Older men are not to be devoted only to their own concerns and pleasure, but are to practice love and faith and patience for others, especially with those of the Christian family. Older women are not to devote themselves to gossip and slanders, over-imbibing in one cocktail party after another. Instead they are to be reverent in behavior, teaching the younger women not to ridicule and belittle their husbands but to love them.

If chastity is a joke to singles and marrieds today, it was not so in the eyes of Jesus and Paul. If fidelity seems prudish and if regarding the other as a whole person instead of a sex object seems out of step with modern times, so be it. So-called "modern times" and their fads have often been out of step with some of the great Christian ideals.

Younger men, says the book of Titus, are to learn to control themselves, even amid the massive stimulation in our society. If youth tend to be passionate and reckless, they should learn self-mastery. How contrary to the popular advice of today where young and old alike are urged to satisfy all lusts and desires without regard to consequences. Ours is an age of instant gratification. Self-discipline in morals is disdained and sexual self-fulfillment is "in." However, many young people learn self-discipline and self-mastery for sports or music or academics. Why should they loathe such discipline in personal behavior? They can gain self-mastery if they wish.

However, seeking love wherever and whenever we can find it soon leads to self-loathing, loneliness, and withdrawal of the real self into a tighter and tighter shell where true intimacy with another human being seems almost impossible. Some years ago Walter Lippmann observed that "the emotion of love, in spite of the romantics, is not self-sustaining; it endures only when the lovers love many things together, and not merely each other. It is this understanding that love cannot necessarily be isolated from the business of living which is the enduring wisdom of the institution of marriage" (*A Preface to Morals*, p. 209).

Some years ago, the noted historian T.R. Glover observed how Jesus changed family life in ancient society. "The heathen," said Glover, "may practice abortion and expose their children and keep parrots instead, but the begetting and bringing up of children is part of the Christian married life" (*Jesus in the Experience of Men*, p. 230). If Christians give more energy to their pets and pleasures than to their families we are indeed in trouble.

To be sure, our industrial, technocratic society focuses on the fulfillment of the individual. The authority and influence of church and parents has been greatly taken over by schools, the state and its agencies, the workplace, peer groups, and the new "knowledge class," of which sociologists Peter and Bridgette Berger speak in their book, *The War over the Family*. Increasingly, the so-called experts advise us that we commonfolk are not wise enough to raise our children, not sage enough to inculcate the important values. And so the family unit is once again fragmented, very often by the very experts who are supposed to keep it together.

Nevertheless, it seems we are desperate for the sense of identity and security and belonging which a good family can give. We have been fascinated with the Mafia movies, in part, I think, because of the strong sense of family and fierce loyalty. They had the assurance they really belonged, even if it was a belonging based on a mingling of terror and love. Many of the communes and cults and authoritarian religions of our time flourish because they give a definite sense of belonging.

But a good Christian family and church can and do provide that important sense of belonging. After all, if we seek our ultimate meaning in the economic sphere, we will be reduced to an economic cipher and be exploited and forgotten and thrown away with the balance sheet. But if we seek our meaning and identity within our family and church, we will find a fulfillment that is more than material, a fulfillment which transcends the ephemeral in hope of the eternal life of the family of God.

The movie *Crimes of the Heart* illustrates by its setting the centrality of family life of yesteryear. The interior of the large family home of the grandfather in Mississippi is decorated for family-centered living and conversation and sharing. More than a stopping off place for food and sleep, the home was the true meeting place of soul with soul. Mutual sharing rather than mutual spectatoring with television was the order of the day.

Home could be a place for sharing concerns and problems. Syndicated columnist Ellen Goodman says her mother was the type "who listened to your problems until you were bored with them."

It is no wonder that the family has become a mere accessory to the many institutions and powers of contemporary life. We have let it become that. But through study, prayer, rescheduling, realignment of priorities, and mutual encouragement and support, the family can take its more rightful place as basic to individual and societal emotional health.

Prayer

Almighty God, Father of our Lord Jesus Christ and our father, who has willed that we should come into life through human birth and who has ordained that we should come to selfhood in relationship with others, we give you thanks for the unique mystery and miracle of life. You have placed the solitary in families and made one generation dependent on the other so as to enrich selfhood and establish community. We are grateful for the heritage of race and family and clan.

God of all peoples, who wills that we should dwell together upon the earth as your cooperative family, we confess our own contributions to hate and hostility. Too often we have been quick to judge and slow to understand. We have been ready to condemn others for their narrowness while failing to recognize our own smallness of mind. We have focused on the follies and foibles of other nations and peoples while emphasizing the strong and pleasing aspects of our own. Forgive our self-righteousness and censoriousness, O Lord. Open us to a deeper and broader understanding of all your people.

Father in heaven, who has created us as your family, look mercifully upon our families with their many needs. Some have experienced the pangs of death. Grant them comfort and your peace which passes understanding. Many are single-parent families suffering not only anger and rejection, but the burden of child-rearing and the challenge of coping all alone. Grant them an extra measure of strength. In some families fathers are at odds with sons and mothers are at odds with daughters. Grant a new breakthrough in communication and understanding.

Loving Father of all, be especially close to those parents whose prodigal children have caused their hearts to be pierced through with many sorrows. Grant strength and comfort to parents and grandparents and others who are alone in the world, so often forsaken and forgotten. Help us to be agents of your love and compassion. And for new parents of little children, for weary parents of adolescents, for parents-in-law and grandparents, we pray an extra measure of your grace that new unity, harmony, and wisdom might be theirs.

In the name of Christ we pray. Amen.

Discussion Questions

1. One highly paid woman executive said she was considering quitting her job, selling their lovely home, and downsizing to live a much simpler and less costly lifestyle in order to spend more time with her husband and family. Would you encourage her to take such drastic action? Are families today too much in debt, living "too high" at too great a cost to family life? Would a simpler, less costly lifestyle be better for families? Worse? What would you advise?

2. Authority in family life seems to be given over to schools, public agencies, institutions, and outside experts, say some observers. Does the family really have any significance in the development of children today? Does the family bear all the responsibility but none of the authority? What changes would you recommend for parents who wish to influence their children?

3. A recent magazine article featured couples who actually looked forward to the workplace, even worked overtime and weekends, because they liked work better than family life. Many parents seem to want little quantity or quality time with their children. Would that be your observation? Are children being neglected by career-oriented parents who shun the responsibilities of parenthood?

Chapter 18

Famlies For The Future

> ... continue in what you have learned
> and have firmly believed, knowing from
> whom you learned it and how from
> childhood you have been associated
> with the sacred writings which are able
> to instruct you for salvation through
> faith in Christ Jesus.
> — 2 Timothy 3:14-15

As we consider what the future might be like for families, it is instructive to note the observations of sociologists regarding marriage and families over the last several decades. In the 1950s, C. Wright Mills, the noted Columbia University sociologist, wrote in his influential book, *The Power Elite*, that the family had taken a subservient role in American life along with schools and churches.

Dr. Mills wrote that "families and churches and schools adapt to modern life; governments and armies and corporations shape it; and as they do so, they turn these lesser institutions into means for their ends" (p. 6). It was the Industrial Revolution that broke up the extended family, he said. Dr. Mills then adds that if the bankruptcy rate among the top five hundred corporations was as high as the divorce rate, there would be economic catastrophe and alarm. Yet this immense social disruption seems to evoke little concern.

Move now from the 1950s to the 1960s, to Charles Reich's best-selling book, *The Greening of America*. He said then that our devotion to the corporate state has produced social separateness, loneliness, and alienation. "America," said Reich, "is one vast, terrifying anti-community." And the family, the most basic social system, "has been ruthlessly stripped to its functional essentials" (p. 7).

Reich goes on to point out that "the family has no work to do together, no mutual education." He notes that the corporate state wants "the family to be a unit for consumption, to exist for the purpose of watching television, using leisure products and services and living the life of false culture" (p. 197).

In the 1970s, the O'Neills, Nena and George, a husband-wife team, published their popular book, *Open Marriage*. They did observe that "divorce now occurs with such frequency that marriage has become a revolving door through which marital partners pass on the way to the next promise of fidelity forever, exchanging one partner for another in a way that makes a mockery of our culture's scorn for polygamy" (p. 82).

Nevertheless, the O'Neills went on to advocate "open marriage," which meant that each partner in a marriage had the right to "grow as an individual within the marriage" (p. 41). "Open marriage is expanded monogamy," they wrote (p. 43), which some interpreted to mean an expanded relationship with someone outside the marriage. To put it plainly, it was an affair with the spouse's consent and best wishes. Indeed, an acquaintance of mine told me he once drove his spouse to a liaison meeting with her lover. The fact that my acquaintance was soon thereafter divorced will give some explanation as to why the O'Neills later modified and retracted their notions of so-called "open marriage."

In the 1980s, sociologists were predicting that most persons would be married three or four times, would have several stepchildren, that there would be a blend of step- and half-brothers and sisters with a confusing conglomerate of dangling grandparents, uncles, aunts, cousins, in-laws, and out-laws.

And in the 1990s, we have some startling observations. In her current book, *Enemies of Eros*, Maggie Gallagher says that "a baby born today stands an almost fifty-fifty chance of being largely abandoned by his father." She says that "father absence and father neglect are being institutionalized on a large scale, by erosion of the mores that discourage illegitimacy and by the collapse of those that discouraged divorce" (p. 111). In the twenty years from 1960 to 1980, single parent families increased from one in eleven to one in five. Now it is estimated that one in four families is single-parent, and that fifty percent of all children under eighteen will have lived in a single-parent home.

But perhaps it was Bob Dylan's song of the 1960s which put it well:

> Come mothers and fathers
> Throughout the land
> And don't criticize
> What you don't understand
> Your sons and daughters
> Are beyond your command
> Your old road is rapidly agin'
> Please get out of the new one
> If you can't lend your hand
> For the times they are a-changin'!*

Indeed they are. But from the Christian point of view, are they changing for the better? What should we hope for in the future for our families?

I.

For one thing, *we need to reaffirm the primacy of family.*

The other day, my wife and I were recalling the advent of special vitamin pills. The enthusiasm was so high at one time, futurist advocates of vitamins were predicting we soon would do away with normal foods. Instead of three meals a day, we might have three or four super vitamins a day. I recall seeing advertisements depicting a beautifully set dinner table with china and silver and three or four pills on each plate. That, we were told, was the wave of the future, the picture of the way it would be. Chefs, culinary institutes, and cookbook publishers beware!

After the 1917 Revolution in Russia, the Marxists advocated free love, allowed divorce and abortion on request, tolerated bigamy, and proposed the state as the all-encompassing, all-sufficient social

---

and economic unit. They believed that arrangement to be the way of the future. The social experiment failed, and in the 1930s marriage and family were re-emphasized. And in 1991, we saw the collapse of the economic and social utopianism of the socialist system.

In our country in the 1960s and 1970s, some writers asserted that group marriage, troikas, and free-love communes would be the wave of the future. But less than one percent experienced that prediction and almost all communes have ceased to exist.

However, today the growing threat to the family is not socialism or communes, but the denigration of both motherhood and fatherhood, says Mrs. Gallagher. She says that "today millions of younger women are trying to live with the system the sixties generation handed down (that's Bob Dylan's generation), coping with the choices they fashioned for us." Millions of women do indeed want their families to be central and primary, but contemporary culture looks down upon a woman who merely wants to manage her home and raise her children. Being a wife, mother, and homemaker is not an "in" choice for today's woman and the family often suffers as a consequence, says Gallagher.

Another phenomenon of the 1990s is the increasingly absent father. Gallagher claims that American society has nearly abolished any significant role for the male in our contemporary families. Children of both sexes seem to be raised predominantly by women, giving children little opportunity to relate positively with men.

The irony of the women's movement is that it has tended to make men *less* responsible for families rather than *more*, says Gallagher. Every mother with children is just a divorce away from welfare. In fact, 54 percent of all single mothers live in poverty (p. 51). Divorced fathers often are excluded from significant relationships with their children, or they exclude themselves, and they consequently are highly negligent in child support. Johnny Carson says that in Hollywood, a faithful husband is one whose alimony check is always on time! Thus, the so-called liberated woman finds herself in an economic and social bondage she was attempting to escape.

Is it any wonder then that American children are doing very badly when their family support system is so fragile or oppressive? About one-fourth of our teenagers drop out of school. Those who do stay and graduate often are functionally illiterate. And those who make it to college usually have to enter remedial reading and math courses just to stay in college.

Children of single-parent families enter into poverty at a high rate. Between 1960 and 1980, juvenile delinquency increased 130 percent. Girls between the ages of fifteen and nineteen had an increase in their illegitimate birth rate of 140 percent, at the same time suffering from an epidemic of sexually transmitted diseases. Between 1973 and 1979, the abortion rate of that same age group jumped 59 percent. The violent death rate for white teenagers skyrocketed and the suicide rate jumped 139 percent, and the rate of teens being murdered 231 percent (*ibid.*, p. 76). All this in the land of the free and the home of the brave where the streets are paved not with gold, but blood.

Is it any wonder then that Gallagher, along with sociologists Peter Berger of Boston University and Brigitte Berger of Wellesley College, argues strongly for the primacy of the family? The Bergers lament the encroachments of the state and quasi-governmental agencies upon the family. They seriously question how an abstract, impersonal agency can replace the love, nurture, and value-formation powers of the family. How can any child find a significant identity with institutions, they ask. The family should be primary.

In a time when society does not reward parents for raising the next generation, parents need to recommit themselves to that task, says Gallagher. The family is a web of relationships wherein we learn who we are and what we can become. "Family is more secure than partnership or friendship," says Gallagher, "precisely because it does not depend on self-interest or mutual affection, though it often generates both. The security of the child rests in knowing that he belongs to his mother and father and that his mother and father belong to him" (*Ibid.*, p. 189).

Indeed, theologian Daniel Day Williams believes the will to belong may be as strong or stronger than the will to power. We have a desperate need to be accepted, to have an identity. Some experts tell us that is one of the appeals of the various cults of today. They appeal to young people because they give them a sense of real belonging, of identity.

Parenting is arduous and at times unpleasant. As Ogden Nash (*I Wouldn't Have Missed It*, Boston: Little, Brown & Co., 1975, p. 35) once put it:

> *Children aren't happy with*
> *nothing to ignore,*
> *And that's what parents*
> *were created for.*

What parent is there who has not wanted to help pack their bags when their teenagers threatened to leave home? Nevertheless, this is the time for mothers and fathers, wives and husbands, parents and children, to affirm each other and the primacy of the family. The corporation or business or state or transitory friendships are poor substitutes for the family unit where we are known, where we belong, or where, when we go there, they have to take us in.

II.

If for the future we need to affirm the primacy of our family, we also need to affirm the *primacy of our religion and its power.*

In lamenting the influence of false teachers and the collapse of principles and values including family values, the author of 2 Timothy also laments the decline of religion. In our text he calls attention to people who are "lovers of pleasure rather than lovers of God, holding the form of religion, but denying the power of it. Avoid such people" (3:4-5).

Moffatt translates the text, noting these people prefer pleasure to God, "for though they keep up a form of religion, they will have nothing to do with it as a force. Avoid all such." Phillips says they maintain a facade of religion, but their conduct will deny its validity. And the *New English Bible* says these are people who put pleasure in the place of God, "men who preserve the outward form of religion, but are a standing denial of its reality. Keep clear of men like these."

196

Americans really need to take a serious look at themselves as to whether they long can endure on the present course. Some years ago, historian Oswald Spengler wrote his seminal book *The Decline of The West*, in which he felt that eventually Europe and America would decline and decay from within because of a loss of the vital powers that sustain a people. Historian Arnold Toynbee acknowledged the possible, even probable decline of the West, but asserted it had within it the powers of regeneration, although his once-mighty British Empire is but a shadow of its former self.

In many ways America is in bad shape. Our education system is behind and deficient. Our infrastructure of roads and bridges is decaying. Our national debt is growing not by simple addition, but exponentially. Violence and crime are everywhere. The conduct of many on Wall Street is characterized in such books as *Den of Thieves, Barbarians at the Gate*, and *Liar's Poker*. I read the other day of a Wall Street billionaire broker who got into his limousine and the chauffeur asked, "Do you want to go to the office first, or should we go right to jail?" We have a deep cynicism about not only our financial institutions, such as Wall Street firms and banks, but also about our government. America is in need of moral and spiritual reform. We need not the form and facade of religion. We need its power.

In the 1700s, Charles and John Wesley, both priests in the Church of England, noted that the poorer classes, especially the coal-miners, were being neglected. So they went to preach the gospel to the poor, the downcast, the neglected and forgotten peoples, who had not even the form of religion. The response was overwhelming. And thus the Methodist Episcopal Church was born in England.

The Wesley brothers, along with George Whitefield and others, decided to bring their message to America. Whitefield led in the Great Awakening of New England and the Middle Atlantic States, which filled the churches to overflowing in the 1730s and 1740s. The Wesleys and their fellow Methodists rode the circuit on the American frontier, establishing hundreds and thousands of churches, to make the Methodists the second largest Protestant denomination in America, second only to the Baptists.

197

The Methodists enjoyed phenomenal growth not so much because of the form of their religion, but because of its power — its power to radically change people's lives for the better. But then John Wesley predicted a day when things would not go so well for religion. "When people gain in wealth and power and comfort, they will begin to neglect their religion," said Wesley. "O yes, they will still go to church, but will find the center of their lives outside the church. And thus the real power of religion will wane because people will believe more in the power of money and pleasure." So prophesied John Wesley.

Wesley was indeed a prophet. Of course we should make money and succeed. Of course we should exercise power and responsibility. But we must remember to keep things in perspective. If we were to ask ourselves about the real center of our lives, what would be our answer? For what do we give ourselves? Our work? Our business? Our corporation? Indeed some today find their total identity in the workplace so that the home and church are merely refueling places for engaging in yet more work. Sometimes we are little more than rats in a treadmill cage, eating, drinking, and sleeping only to turn the wheels of business faster.

That is why our author urges Timothy to remember the scriptures taught to him by his mother and grandmother. It was in the context of a loving family that he learned the values and principles which have an eternal dimension. In the surroundings of a friendly genetic heritage and supportive environment, Timothy was taught to avoid the fads and fancies which come and go as one money-making scheme after another.

Contrary to the popular teachers of his day, who flattered their hearers and pandered to their whims and passions, Timothy was to look to the scriptures, which were bold to correct, to reprove, to teach, and to train so that the people of God would not be duped and suckered into one hurtful vanity after another.

Timothy, with all the church, was to center his life on God as revealed in the sacred scriptures. If the religious teachers promised only to make them comfortable, if they preached a message which put God at their disposal rather than themselves at God's disposal, if they merely entertained without asking for commitment and involvement, then avoid them, says our author. It is a form of religion without power.

Families for the future? You bet. We need to affirm them and help them and sustain them for their sake and our nation's sake. Families for the future? Yes indeed. They will survive if we and our nation reaffirm our true spiritual center. Money and pleasure make poor gods in the end. Only the true God can bring us into a truly satisfying future.

Prayer

Almighty God, who dwells beyond the farthest reaches of outer space, whose Being encompasses the universe, and yet whose presence is to be found in the tiniest and most concentrated of inner spaces, everywhere we look we see the traces of your handiwork, and each piece of reality we examine leads to awe and wonder and worship of your greater reality. Praise be to you, our Lord God, for all your creative wonders.

If the world astounds us with wonder and mystery, perhaps even more are we astounded by the wonder and mystery of ourselves. Entranced as we sometimes are with the unconscious world, we even more are entranced with our own self-conscious world. You have made us in your image, with capacities for love and creativity, thinking and deciding. And yet what dark powers work within our psyche — the powers of greed and lust, of hate and revenge; the powers of fear and malice, envy and even murder itself. O God, we sense that we ourselves, in our inmost being, are the battlefield whereon the forces of good and evil conduct their eternal struggle. And we confess that much too often we let the evil within us have its way. We ask for your forgiveness, O God.

Hear us then as we come to you for aid in our struggle for truth within ourselves and with one another. Grant us strength to overcome the forces that hurt and destroy. Save us from destructive criticism and the cancer of negativism. Cleanse our souls of grudges so long held they eat away at our hearts like acid, destroying us more than our enemies. Free our minds from ideas that bind more than liberate, from thoughts that confine, rather than release, from perceptions which cloud the truth rather than reveal it, from prejudices which fester with fear and ignorance rather than with sympathetic knowledge which leads to understanding.

And for our families we especially pray. See what forces work to tear us apart, to alienate and offend. Help us to be open to one another, to communicate well, to let go the grudges and long-remembered wrongs, to be tenderhearted, to forgive one another, even as Christ has forgiven our offenses, cleanse us, heal us, and make us whole, we pray.

Through Jesus Christ our Lord. Amen.

Discussion Questions

1. The feminist revolution has displaced the husband and father in contemporary culture, say some observers. Men and their concerns have been pushed to the side and even are scorned. Consequently, we have the absent father syndrome more and more. Do you agree or disagree with these observations? What might be done to encourage men to be more responsible husbands and fathers?

2. Some claim that the increase of success and wealth leads to the breakdown of true religion and sincere spirituality. Couples and families come to rely more on what money can buy for them than upon authentic religious development. Are success and wealth a detriment to genuine marriage and family life or an asset? Conversely, do failure and poverty adversely affect families and marriages or bring them closer together? How should Christian families be advised in coping with either wealth or lack of money?

3. Is the deterioration of family life signalling the deterioration of the American civilization, as some critics suggest? What three basic recommendations would you make for the improvement of American family life?

Chapter 19

Marriage And The Home Improvement Committee

*"Honor your father and mother"(this is the first
commandment with a promise), "that it may
be well with you and that you may live long on the
earth."*
                                                — Ephesians 6:2-3

It is risky putting two somewhat unpopular concepts in a title
— concepts like marriage and committee. Neither one receives
especially good press these days. Everyone knows that a camel is
a horse created by a committee. Stewart Harol says a committee is
a group of the unfit, appointed by the unwilling to do the unneces-
sary. And every politician knows the way to dodge a potentially
explosive issue is to give it to a committee to study for two or three
years until the issue is forgotten.

Marriage also receives bad press. This wedding announcement
appeared recently in a local newspaper: "Jack Jones and Pamela
Smith were married on Saturday, thus ending a friendship that began in their school days."

If marriage is perceived by many to be the end of friendship, it
is perceived by many others to be the end of romance. At the pub
the other night, Al announced to his friends that they now have an
organization called Marriage Anonymous. When you feel like getting married, you call somebody and he sends over a woman with
curlers in her hair and cream on her face, wearing a torn housecoat
and claiming she has a headache!

The younger generation is probably more in tune with Sylvia
and Ruth. Since it was leap year, Sylvia asked Ruth if she was
proposing to Charlie. Ruth said, "No — my feelings toward him
have changed." Sylvia asked, "Then will you return his diamond

ring?" Ruth said, "No — my feelings toward the diamond ring have not changed."

Nevertheless, despite broken engagements, marriage does remain popular. Most people who live together eventually get married. And most people who get divorced remarry, some for the third or fourth time. Nevertheless, as many have said, "Remarriage is the triumph of hope over experience."

But there is another word in the title besides *committee* and *marriage*. It is the word *home*, implying family. And homes and families have also suffered in these times. There is a growing concern that the disintegration of the family is signaling a disintegration of the nation and civilization. Even the phrase "family values" has become controversial. Some deride the phrase as a conservative political ploy to return America to a nostalgic past, whereas others use the phrase to affirm the importance of stable family life for the future of our civilization.

Nevertheless, marriage and family have been at the center of religion for centuries. And lately committees and committees within committees with meetings within meetings have come to prominence in most churches. Therefore, it might seem appropriate for the church to address the topic, "Marriage and the Home Improvement Committee."

In keeping with the Judeo-Christian religious tradition of nearly four thousand years, I would like to suggest two members for the committee from our sacred past. As we invite them forward to the committee meeting, we'll ask each of them to say a few words about marriage and home improvement.

I.

Our first committee member is the venerable *Moses*, the *great* law*giver*.

As he comes forward, let me remind you of a few important items from his past — items which he would be too modest to mention, because, as was said of him, he was a meek man, meekest in all the earth. You will recall he was raised in the home of the most powerful man on earth — the Pharaoh of the Egyptians.

Yet the power and prestige of that upbringing did not prevent him from identifying with his own enslaved and oppressed people, the Hebrews. He got into trouble defending a Hebrew slave and escaped to save his life. But it was this same Moses when God called back to lead the Hebrews in the famous Exodus from Egypt. It was this same Moses who led them through the Red Sea waters, and this very same Moses who received on Mount Sinai, in person, the Ten Commandments, direct from the hand of God himself. So we feel extremely fortunate to have Moses speak directly to us from the marriage and home improvement committee. Welcome, Moses.

Thank you very much. I'm glad to be here. The first thing I want to do is to tell you what God told me on Mount Sinai. Here was his fifth commandment: "Honor your father and mother, so that you may live long on the earth." In many societies in my time the children were disrespectful, rebellious, disobedient, callous, and without sincere human affection. Children of all times must learn to honor their parents. A stable family life with proper respect for authority and order is key to the survival of any society or culture.

God intended not just for young children to honor their parents, but for adult children to honor and respect their aging parents. In my time many people took their elderly out into the wilderness, and abandoned them to die of starvation and exposure, finally to be eaten by the wild beasts.

I've noticed that today in your society people put their elderly parents in a nursing home (which can be good), and never again go to see them. They just abandon them. That's not the way of God. If you lose respect for your aging parents, it's often because of your own selfishness and greed. You don't want to be inconvenienced.

And now that the roles are switched, where the children become the parents and the parents become the children, the offspring don't want the responsibility. Without gratitude for the help they received in childhood, they now refuse to help their parents in their "second childhood." Before you know it, children will be encouraging their parents toward assisted suicide, without much thought, or toward euthanasia, without much thought, so they won't have to be bothered with them. But you are to "honor your father and mother" so that their lives and yours may be long upon the earth. It is the law of God.

Thank you, Moses. You are coming through loud and clear. Is there anything else you have to say?

Yes, there is, as a matter of fact. It's something I've been saying for centuries, and yet it never quite seems to sink in. I've been telling parents that it is their responsibility to teach their children the commandments of God and the important spiritual values.

Parents try to put that responsibility solely on the shoulders of the priests, rabbis and ministers. They do have that responsibility, but so do the parents. Parents are to teach their children diligently that the Lord their God is one; and that they should love God with all their heart and soul and strength and mind.

I've noticed from my perspective how easily God gets displaced by other gods. Sex was big-time in Baalism in Canaan and it's a big-time fascination and moneymaker in America. Money itself always competes with God for first place. And if in the Middle Ages the cathedral was the real and symbolic center of life, and if in New England the church was central on the town square, the school and university now occupy those locations of exalted importance.

People have forgotten that they also are to love God with their mind. Parents want to make sure their children eat right, get their vitamins, and brush their teeth. They are concerned to get them into the right nursery schools, so as to get them into the right prep schools, so as to get them into the right colleges and graduate schools, so as to launch them in the right careers. But they totally neglect Bible and theology and philosophy. Spiritual development and character formation are way down the list in importance from S.A.T. scores and academic achievement.

God doesn't have anything against these. It is just that parents often neglect the deepest and most important dimension of the human being — the spiritual. My suggestion is that we could go a long way toward improving marriage and family if children honored their parents, and parents in turn honored their children by teaching them the commandments and values of God, because, well, they are eternal.

206

II.

Thank you, Moses. What a privilege it has been to have you here again. For our next committee member, we come this way in time about fourteen hundred years, to the first century of our era. And we would like to ask the *Apostle Paul* to say a few words about *marriage and home improvement*.

While he is coming forward and preparing to speak, let me remind you of some of his background. Paul grew up in Tarsus, a city on the southeast coast of what is now Turkey. He attended the university there and then went on to Jerusalem to be taught by the famous Jewish teacher, Gamaliel.

Paul, whose Hebrew name was Saul, was Jewish, with an impeccable genealogy. He was of the prestigious tribe of Benjamin and probably grew up in a fairly well-to-do family. Although we know he had a sister and nephew, he never tells us anything about his parents. He experienced a radical conversion after the living Christ appeared to him, and as a consequence, he became one of the leading forces in the spread of Christianity into a universal religion. In fact, Christ kept appearing to him, inspiring him with the message of God. Welcome, Paul. How good of you to come to be with us!

Thank you for inviting me to speak on the subject of improving marriage and the home. I must confess right away something that many of you already know — namely, that I never married and I never had children. I know your minister is accustomed to saying, with respect to advice for raising children, that at one time he had no children and plenty of advice, but now has six children and no advice.

No doubt, he will put me in that category — no children and lots of advice! And I suppose the married people could say the same thing — what does he know about marriage? He's never had a wife. Some scholars think I must have been unhappily married because I kept praying to God to be rid of that "thorn in my side." That did not refer to a wife, but to a physical ailment!

Nevertheless, even though I was never married, I was celibate, and believed that was what God wanted me to be. However, I preached strongly against fornication and adultery and taught the

207

importance of sincere love and fidelity between husband and wife. I taught again and again that love is not just a matter of emotions and feelings, but a matter of the will. A stable marriage and family cannot be built on moods and whims and selfishness. It needs the solid rock of commitment.

But with respect to the family, I want to echo my great teacher, Moses, and say that children must learn to obey their parents so that it might be well with you and them and that you might live long on the earth.

However, I must hasten to clarify myself. It is probable that some of you acquainted with history are thinking of the Roman society of my century. In my time, a Roman father had what was called *patria potestas*, "father power," which meant the father had absolute power over his children. He could make them work for him, sell them into slavery, even put them to death, although that was rarely done.

Girls came off the worst, as did the sickly and deformed. As late as 7 A.D., the Emperor Augustus banished his adulterous daughter, Julia, and had her infant child killed. In the year just before Christ, a man named Hilarion wrote his wife, Alis, saying, "If — good luck to you — you have a child, if it is a boy, let it live; if it is a girl, throw it out." Unwanted children were regularly left in the forum to be sold as slaves or raised as prostitutes.

So I want to assure you children that I have nothing like that in mind. I have never advocated the idea of *patria potestas*. However, it seems to me that in America it has become just the opposite. Instead of the parents having the power, the children now seem to have it.

Many parents seem to have a craving to be loved by their children, rather than respected. They seem afraid of the children, afraid the children will reject them, so they give them everything, indulge them, spoil them. The rumor is that some parents even provide the beer for their teenage children's keg parties or provide hotel rooms in Manhattan for their enjoyment. Many parents seem to be afraid of their children, afraid they won't be liked and accepted by them. So they try to be buddies with their children instead of being parents.

That's why I'd like to say again as I said to the Ephesians nineteen centuries ago, that you fathers (and mothers) should bring up your children in the discipline and instruction of the Lord. I think you fathers have a special role here — the role of discipline you often leave to the mothers.

And by discipline I don't mean a harshness and severity that provokes your children to anger and exasperation so they get the sense they never can please you. Be careful about unreal expectations. One father said, "My son, when Abraham Lincoln was your age, he believed so much in education, he walked twelve miles to school." The son replied, "Yes, but, Dad, when Abraham Lincoln was your age, he was President!"

Be careful about unreal expectations. But I'd like to urge the fathers to have the courage to stand up to their children, to join with other fathers to say we're not going to tolerate uncivil, irreligious, disrespectful behavior. Be put on warning, we are not always going to side with your misbehavior and say the police and school authorities are always wrong and you are always right. We may have the money to buy you out of trouble, but you may have to pay for the consequences of your misdeeds.

For example, I read an alarming article in a recent *New York* magazine about "Teenage Gangland" (December 16, 1996, p. 32ff) where rich Manhattan teenagers are teaming up with ghetto teenagers to sell drugs to rich prep-school students. They cruise in their rented luxury cars, sell drugs and do drugs, drink beer, crash and burglarize apartments of rich friends when their parents are away.

These rich teenage gangsters claim they sell drugs to sons and daughters of some of New York's richest and most famous. "We are like *gods* to kids," boasted one gangster leader. "V.I.P.s at every club know us," he boasted. "Promoters use us. Superstar kids know who we are. People like us are gonna be the people other people look up to."

Well, maybe. But probably not if these rich and famous parents get their acts together and start to pay more attention to their children than to themselves. Many parents just can't be bothered with their children. They are pursuing their careers, arranging their social calendars, planning their extended vacations, leaving children home alone with a housekeeper.

My advice is centuries-old, but I think it's still relevant. Children and young people need instruction, not just in math, but in morals. They need to learn not only how to put a sentence together, but also how to put a meaningful life together. If parents support the disciplines necessary for their music, academic, and athletic achievement, they should also support the disciplines necessary for their spiritual, moral, and character achievement. Computer people have a saying, "Garbage in, garbage out." Parents need to understand the same thing is true with children. Put garbage into their minds and hearts and souls and you'll get garbage out. I think that American Christians need to renew their commitment to marriage and family.

This is about it for now. I would go on, but ever since years ago when I preached late into the night and Eutychus dozed off and fell out of the upstairs window, I have been skittish about long sermons. I'll have more to say the next time.

Thank you, Moses and Paul, for your inspired words which come powerfully to us across the centuries.

And now as the convener of the committee I would like to offer a few practical tips on marriage and family. First, be sure to spend prime time together when you are not preoccupied or exhausted. Second, try to eat together regularly and say grace. And then listen to each other, television off. Be truly interested in each other's life.

Third, express affection. I like what one young mother does with her young children. At the end of each day, they just sit together and spend five minutes hugging and talking. A hug a day keeps the divorce attorney away. And lastly, make Church and Sunday School and Bible reading and studying and prayer a regular part of your disciplined life — like the young family I see here every Sunday, early, three children, bathed and dressed, and ready to learn more than they'll ever know. At age fifty, they will look back and thank their parents for the disciplines of spiritual life which formed the foundation of their lives.

Well, that's about it for the marriage and home improvement committee. May God bless you in your marriage and home.

Prayer

Almighty God, Creator of the universe and our Creator, who has chosen to express yourself in millions of galaxies and then to focus yourself in humankind, we praise you for bringing us forth in your image. Out of the depths of your being you have manifested yourself in our masculinity and femininity. And in the erotic gender dance of the whole earth, you create the dynamism of passion and the mysteries of love. You entice us with the overwhelming delights of sensual pleasure to assure the continuance of the human race even through the pain of childbirth and tragedies of human freedom. And in our coming together — masculine and feminine — the circle of your divine love is completed. We thank you.

If the pleasure of love and life is enthralling, the pain and heartache of the living of these days sometimes are overwhelming. Tensions and hostilities exist within many families. Children are set against the parents and parents against the children. Misunderstandings abound. Callouses cover an assaulted heart. Indifference chills like a New England fog, and people become strangers to one another in their own house, in their own family.

That is why we come to you, loving Father, to receive inspiration and wisdom and strength to break the emotional gridlock. We so much want to love and be loved, to share, to understand and to be understood. How much our souls long for a true intimacy, an authentic togetherness, a deeply satisfying love which liberates rather than smothers.

Be pleased to help us, to come to us in your kindly mercy and compassion, to aid us in our loving. Turn the hearts of parents and children toward each other, and bring us all closer to you to know the richness of your gracious kindness and the delights of your divine way of life.

Through Jesus Christ our Lord. Amen.

Discussion Questions

1. Many middle-age couples find themselves in the "sandwich generation," squeezed between responsibilities for their children and for their parents who may be into their "second childhood." How do couples in this situation properly honor their parents? Is it appropriate to put them in nursing homes? Should they bring them into their own homes to live with them? What would you suggest?

2. Some parents seem to want to be "buddies" and "friends" with their children, seeking their approval and acceptance rather than exercising parenting responsibilities. Critics claim this is unhealthy, that parents need to be parents of their children, not "buddies." What do you think?

3. Public schools cannot teach religion and morals. The responsibility therefore rests on churches and families. How might families develop ways to teach their children religious and moral values? What methods or activities might they utilize? Which should they avoid? What three disciplines could be helpful in improving family life?

Chapter 20

"The Second Time Around"

Let all bitterness and wrath and anger and clamor
and slander be put away from you, with all malice,
and be kind to one another, forgiving one another,
as God in Christ forgave you.
— Ephesians 4:31-32

Perhaps no American singer has touched as many human emotions as that one-time boy from, of all places, Hoboken, New Jersey, Frank Sinatra. And possibly few American singers have had the success of "Ol' Blue Eyes," spanning the generations with ballads of love and romance, betrayal and forgiveness, estrangement and reconciliation. It was as if he and his songwriters reached into the secret places of millions of hearts to frame our emotions in unforgettable tunes and words and rhythms.

And how many of us have taken heart as we listened to him croon these soothing words, "Love is lovelier the second time around"? He goes on to sing of love with "both feet on the ground," admitting love might be wasted on the young. It may seem that love comes but once, yet he's "glad we met, the second time around."

This beautiful song flies directly in the face of the old adage that "a second marriage is the triumph of hope over experience." And this song is treated at first with scorn by women and men so abused in the first marriage, so disgruntled and disheartened, so betrayed and misunderstood, they vow, "never again."

And yet as time goes by, as the nights get longer, and the weekends get lonelier, and they hear again the beloved Frankie on the stereo, they begin to think perhaps "love is lovelier, the second time around, just as wonderful with both feet on the ground."

As a matter of fact, more and more people are giving love and marriage a "second time around." At least one out of two marriages ends in divorce, and according to a University of Wisconsin study, that number may be as high as two out of three marriages ending in divorce.

A lot of people are divorcing, and of those divorcing, the great majority remarry for a second and even a third time. Although second and third marriages have an even higher failure rate than first marriages, remarriage is, as we have said, "the triumph of hope over experience." It is the hope that Sinatra is correct, that "love is more comfortable the second time you fall, Like a friendly home the second time you call." However, divorce is not the only occasion for second marriage. Many are widowed at various stages and often are confronted with the question of remarriage.

Then there are those that have had live-in arrangements that are much like common-law marriages, and they break up. And don't most marriages — first, second or third — need the opportunity for a "second time around"? So what factors should we consider for the second time around?

I.

For one thing, we need to accept the probability, even the necessity, for a second time around.

Over the years I have married many couples who have been living together — the majority these days doing so before marriage. And I have married many widows and widowers, and I have united many in marriage who have been divorced.

Those who come to me from a Roman Catholic or conservative Protestant background sometimes wonder why I, like many Protestant ministers, marry people who have been divorced. Do we have different Bibles with different teachings regarding divorce and remarriage? they sometimes ask.

Of course we read the same Bible where Jesus seems strongly to condemn divorce except in the cases of adultery. And we read the same Gospels where Jesus says divorced persons who remarry are committing adultery. Saint Paul, never a favorite with women, seems to permit divorce of an "unbelieving partner" and even hints at the legitimacy of remarriage of divorced people. Yet over the centuries, the Church's official stance usually has been against divorce.

214

Recall that even King Henry VIII of England could not get a divorce granted by the Pope so he could marry Anne Boleyn. So he split from the Church of Rome, made himself head of the Church of England, and thus obtained his divorce. Even today, the Church of Rome will not grant divorce, although it will go through the highly questionable procedure of annulment, claiming a true marriage never took place. Yes, making the claim even though several children may be running around to prove the marriage was indeed consummated.

Some Protestant churches are nearly as bad. I recall one Protestant divorced couple who came to me for marriage because their rather conservative minister would not, on scruple, marry divorced people. However, he told them once they were married they would be most welcome into the full membership of his church. So I married them and they returned to his church, the inconsistency of that approach never dawning on them.

I must confess Jesus' teaching on divorce and remarriage is a bit of a mystery to me. He and the New Testament writers assert forgiveness and a second chance for thieves, rapists, embezzlers, extortioners, frauds, hypocrites, adulterers, but not, it would appear, for divorcées. Why, I ask myself, should not people who have failed in marriage be given a second chance just as people who have failed in integrity or civility? Why does the Church forgive Mafia types, burying them from the Church, even, while they forbid divorce and refuse to marry a divorcée within the Church?

If Christianity is anything, it is second chance religion, the religion of beginning again, the religion of forgiveness and restitution, the religion of grace triumphing over judgment and mercy winning out over condemnation.

I tell divorced people that I marry them because I believe in forgiveness, in giving the life back to start over again, in helping people to rise above regret and alienation, above hostility and estrangement to experience acceptance and wholeness. I tell divorced people that if divorce is failure — and it is failure of one kind or another — then Christianity is here to help us succeed. I tell doubtful divorced people that if divorce is sin — and in many ways sin is involved in divorce — then Christ died to save sinners, to make them whole, to help them begin again. Yes, because of Christ it can be true that, love will be lovelier the second time around.

II.

But if we accept the probability of the second time around, we need also to accept the responsibilites of the second time around.

That is the theme of our text from Ephesians. Typical of the Pauline format, this Letter to the Christians in Ephesus argues the theology of the Christian Faith in the first half, and then in the second half, gives the ethical and practical implications of the theology just stated. Briefly put, the author says that since we have been made new in Christ, since we have been given a second chance with God, we should behave in second chance ways, in new ways.

As my friend Ernie Campbell says of the Prodigal Son in Jesus' famous story, after the welcome home party is over the son is expected to take on the responsibilites of sonship. So too in a second time around marriage, there are responsibilites.

One responsibility is to dispel faulty assumptions. Just as people marry the first time with important and unspoken assumptions regarding hopes and expectations, so do they often marry the second time with unarticulated assumptions. One woman, into her second marriage a year or so, told me one day she woke up to realize her second husband was quite a different man than her first husband. She assumed he would behave about like her first husband, but he behaved quite differently, and she wasn't sure she liked it.

People in second marriages sometimes find themselves calling their second partner by the first partner's name. Very often, they play the same emotional tapes, expecting the partner to play a role similar to the first partner. Expectations regarding lovemaking, dining, household habits and chores, money, vacations, children and holidays often have not been articulated. Just as first marriages often fail because of unspoken assumptions, so do second and third marriages fail even more for the same reason. "Love may be comfortable, the second time you fall," especially if you have learned to express your feelings, hopes, and expectations in understandable and agreeable ways.

Another responsibility for the second time around and any time around is that of forgiveness. Sooner or later we need to let go of our hatred and hostility and anger at the divorced partner. Let it go. Just as God forgave us in Christ and got rid of the grudge against us, so we need to forgive our ex-spouse as Christ forgives our failures.

Richard Fitzgibbons, a psychiatrist in suburban Philadelphia, says spiritual forgiveness is sometimes the only way to relieve deep hurts. He says, "If there is really deep, deep betrayal and anger, people are limited in their ability to let go of their anger even if they're intellectually able to understand it." That's where they need the spiritual help of Christ. Bill McCartney, one-time popular coach of the University of Colorado football team, and now the founder of the nationwide men's movement, Promise Keepers, relates how bad his marriage was until he made a radical change. His wife Lyndi suffering through her husband's affair and neglect, says, "When you're able to forgive like the Lord forgives, it sets you free" (*Newsday*, 1-10-97, p. B3).

Indeed it does. Studies show forgiveness improves both psychological and physical health. Grudge bearing and a wish for vengeance often destroy the person carrying them rather than destroying the object of their anger. Let it go. Forgive as Christ forgave you, says the author of Ephesians.

And then we must, the second time or any time around, take responsibility for good habits in marriage. Psychologist Dr. John Gottman (*Why Marriages Succeed or Fail*) says we need to avoid four bad habits that sabotage a marriage or relationship. One bad habit is criticism. While complaint is common in marriage and sometimes helpful, criticism usually heaps blame on the partner and passes judgment on him or her as being inferior with serious flaws in character. A complaint says how I feel about a situation and avoids the universal, global accusations of "you always" and "you never."

A worse bad habit to avoid is contempt, says Dr. Gottman. With contempt we intend to insult, to heap abuse on our partners with name calling, hostile humor, and mockery. Counteract this tendency with a firm resolve to name those things you admire in your

217

partner. What were the good things that brought you together in the first place? Talk about them and affirm them.

Another bad habit is that of defensiveness. In the defensive mode we become stubborn, deny responsibility, make excuses, and cross-complain. Imagine this dialogue:

Pamela: "Once again you didn't pay the credit card on time and now we will have to pay a penalty. I don't know what happened to me that I should end up with such an irresponsible man."

Eric: "Listen, it was your turn to pay the bills this month, not mine."

Pamela: "So now you're going to lie to get out of this just like other times?"

Eric: "You're the liar! Last month we agreed it would be your turn to handle the bills this month."

Pamela: "That's because you're too irresponsible to be trusted with them. I wasn't supposed to start paying till next month."

Eric: "Get it right. You're wrong!"

Pamela: "You're so full of it."

Now consider this alternative dialogue:

Pamela: "I notice that you didn't pay the credit card on time, so now we have to pay a penalty."

Eric: "I thought it was your turn to pay the bills this month, not mine."

Pamela: "No, remember we agreed you would pay the bills this month."

Eric: "I understood it differently. Sorry. Perhaps we should write down a schedule so we don't have this mix-up again. I'll go ahead and pay the bill. Sorry about the penalty."

To break out of stubbornness and defensiveness, Dr. Gottman recommends you try to see your partner's complaints not as an attack, but as information being strongly expressed! Hard to do to be sure, but try to empathize and understand your partner.

Another bad habit is that of stonewalling. Most stonewallers (85 percent of them are men) think they are neutralizing the situation by saying nothing. Yet they actually communicate disapproval or smugness or an icy distance, says Gottman. Physiologically men's heart rate and blood pressure go up more in conflict than in women and men often cope by stonewalling. Thus they and their spouse should allow a cooling off period before trying to resolve a conflict.

So what are some positive strategies? One is to calm down. Take a time out. Walk around the block. Be angry and sin not, as our text says. But don't let the sun set on your anger. Don't go to bed without resolution of the argument unless, like one couple, you don't go to bed for seven nights! Avoid excessive alcohol, take a breather, and then communicate in a calmer frame of mind.

Another strategy, says Gottman, is to speak non-defensively. Reintroduce praise and admiration for your spouse even if you have to do it through tight lips. You can be the architect of your thoughts and comments and you can choose to emphasize the positive more than the negative. Most all of us are more ready to change in a climate of acceptance and affirmation than in a climate of hostility and negativity.

A further strategy is that of validation. Instead of attacking the partner's point of view try to hear what he or she is feeling. It's a matter of empathy, or as our Biblical text puts it, "Let no evil talk come out of your mouths." Instead use language that builds up rather than tears down.

And the last and first strategy for the second time around, and for any time around, is that of heartfelt love.

You may recall the report in the news media of the Palestinian boy who was killed by an Israeli soldier. His body was rushed to the hospital, but to no avail, and the surgeons asked the parents if they would be willing to donate their son's vital organs to needy persons. The parents responded yes.

Should the organs, asked the surgeons, be used only in Arab candidates or in Israeli candidates as well? In anyone who needs them, said the Arab parents. And so the organs of an Arab boy were implanted in the bodies of Israeli enemies – an Arab heart beating in a Jewish child – the second time around. The Song of Solomon is right, "Love is stronger than death ... Many waters (of sorrow) cannot quench love."

And so it should be with us in our marriages — our heart beating, as it were, in the being of our beloved, with empathy and understanding and vitality. Then we'll be glad we met "the second time around."

Prayer

Almighty God, source of all life, who has been pleased to set in motion the vital forces of all living things, and who has made the world a stage for the interplay of the male and female erotic dance from insects to elephants, we give you thanks and praise for this mysterious gift of sexual desire and this almost desperate longing for love. It is the heartbeat of the world, and in it we sense that you, as well as ourselves, are coming to fulfillment and completion.

It is only natural then we should bring to you, Divine Author of love, our frustrations in loving. We are so often lonely, so thwarted in our longing to love and be loved. Often we misunderstand not only our partner, but ourselves. Help us come to greater insight and expanded maturity. Liberate us from hang-ups and false notions. Bring us to greater wholeness in loving.

We pray especially for those divorced or widowed or separated. Grant them strength in loneliness and help in anger or grief. And for those in marriage for a second time, or a third time, we pray a new measure of grace and understanding for the adjustments to be made and wisdom for the accommodations to new realities.

And for us all in our loving, we pray refreshment from your life-giving Spirit and vitality from your heart of love which pulses in us all. Through Jesus Christ our Lord. Amen.

Discussion Questions

1. Many churches believe divorce (except in certain circumstances) is a sin. Are there times when divorce is better than the continuation of a marriage? Or should the marriage vows be maintained at all costs? Why? Why not?

2. Some Christian groups permit divorce but not remarriage. Are they more faithful to the teachings of the Bible than those who remarry persons who have been divorced? Why? Why not?

3. Is a second marriage significantly different from the first? Should it be? What helpful advice might be given to those contemplating a second (or third) marriage or those already in a second marriage?

Bibliography

Achtemeier, Elizabeth, *The Committed Marriage*, Philadelphia, PA, Westminster Press, 1976.

Avis, Paul, *Eros and the Sacred*, Harrisburg, PA, Morehouse Publishing, 1990.

Bach, Dr. George R. and Wyden, Peter, *The Intimate Enemy*, New York, NY, Avon Books, 1968.

Bellah, Robert N., *The Good Society*, New York, NY, Alfred A. Knopf, 1991.

Bellah, Robert N.; Madsen, Richard; Sullivan, William M.; Swidler, Ann; and Tipton, Steven M., *Habits of the Heart*, Berkeley, CA, University of California Press, 1985.

Benjamin, Jessica, *The Bonds of Love*, New York, NY, Pantheon Books, 1988.

Berger, Brigitte and Peter L., *The War Over the Family*, Garden City, NY, Anchor Press/Doubleday, 1983.

Bible, The, Revised Standard Version Bible.

Bloom, Allan, *The Closing of the American Mind*, New York, NY, Simon & Schuster, 1987.

Bloomfield, Dr. Harold and Vettese, Sirah, Ph.D., *Lifemates*, New York, NY, New American Library, 1989.

Bly, Robert, *Iron John*, Reading, MA, Addison-Wesley Publishing, 1990.

Bombeck, Erma, *Family: The Ties That Bind — and Gag!*, Boston, MA, G.K. Hall, 1987.

Bower, Robert, *Solving Problems in Marriage*, Grand Rapids, MI, William B. Eerdmans Publishing, 1972.

Brenton, Myron, *The American Male*, London, England, George Allen and Unwin, Ltd., 1967.

Brown, Norman O., *Love's Body,* New York, NY, Random House, 1966.

Cabot, Richard C., *Christianity and Sex*, New York, NY, Macmillan Co., 1938.

Christensen, James L., *Before Saying "I Do,"* Old Tappan, NJ, Fleming H. Revell Co., 1983.

Clinebell, Howard J. and Charlotte H., *The Intimate Marriage*, New York, NY, Harper & Row, 1970.

Dawn, Marva J., *Sexual Character*, Grand Rapids, MI, William B. Eerdmans Publishing, 1993.

de Rougemont, Denis, *Love in the Western World*, Princeton, NJ, Princeton University Press, 1983.

Dittes, James, E., *The Male Predicament*, San Francisco, CA, Harper & Row, 1985.

Duvall, Evelyn M. and Sylvanus M., *Sex Ways — in Fact and Faith*, New York, NY, Association Press, 1961.

Fitch, Robert E., *Of Love and Suffering*, Philadelphia, PA, Westminster Press, 1970.

Fromm, Erich, *The Art of Loving*, New York, NY, Harper & Row, 1956.

Gallagher, Maggie, *Enemies of Eros*, Chicago, IL, Bonus Books, 1989.

Geiger, H. Kent, *Comparative Perspectives on Marriage and the Family*, Boston, MA, Little, Brown & Co., 1968.

Genne, Elizabeth and William H., *Christians and the Crisis in Sex Morality*, New York, NY, Association Press, 1962.

Gittlesohn, Roland B., *Love, Sex and Marriage: A Jewish View,* New York, NY, Union of American Hebrew Congregations, 1990.

Glieberman, Herbert A., *Closed Marriage*, Kansas City, KS, Sheed Andrews & McMeel, Inc., 1978.

Glover, T.R., *Jesus In the Experience of Men*, London, England, Student Christian Movement, 1921.

Gordis, Robert, *Love and Sex: A Modern Jewish Perspective*, New York, NY, Farrar Straus Giroux, 1978.

Gottman, John, *Why Marriages Succeed or Fail*, New York, NY, Simon & Schuster, Inc., 1994.

Gray, John, Ph.D., *Men Are From Mars, Women Are From Venus*, New York, NY, Harper Collins, 1992.

Gray, John, *Men, Women and Relationships, Making Peace With the Opposite Sex*, Hillsboro, OR, Beyond Words Publishing, Inc., 1993.

Highwater, Jamake, *Myth and Sexuality*, New York, NY, Penguin Books, 1990.

Hill, Langdon, *Mr. Romance's Book of Love*, Tucson, AZ, Knight-Ridder Press, 1986.

Hiltner, Seward, *Sex and the Christian Life*, New York, NY, Association Press, 1957.

Hodgson, Leonard, *Sex and Christian Freedom*, Naperville, IL, SCM Press, 1967.

Holstege, Henry, *The Christian Family, Occasional Papers From Calvin College,* Grand Rapids, MI, 1988.

Janus, Samuel S. and Cynthia L., *The Janus Report on Human Sexuality*, New York, NY, John Wiley & Sons, 1993.

Johnson, Edwin Clark, *In Search of God in the Sexual Underworld*, New York, NY, William Morrow & Co., 1983.

Johnson, Robert A., *He: Understanding Masculine Psychology*, New York, NY, Harper & Row Publishers, 1974.

Katz, Dr. Stan J. and Liu, Aimee E., *False Love*, New York, NY, Ticknor & Fields, 1988.

Keen, Sam, *The Passionate Life: Stages of Loving*, San Francisco, CA, Harper & Row Publishers, 1983.

Kennedy, Eugene C., *The New Sexuality*, Garden City, NY, Image Books, 1973.

Kierkegaard, Soren, *Works of Love*, New York, NY, Harper & Row, 1962.

Klagsbrun, Francine, *Married People: Staying Together in the Age of Divorce*, New York, NY, Bantam Books, 1985.

Kriegel, Leonard, *On Men and Manhood*, New York, NY, Hawthorn Books, 1979.

Lasch, Christopher, *The Culture of Narcissism*, New York, NY, W. W. Norton & Co., 1978.

L'Engle, Madeleine, *The Irrational Season*, San Francisco, CA, Harper & Row Publishers, 1979.

L'Engle, Madeleine, *Two Part Invention*, San Francisco, CA, Harper & Row Publishers, 1988.

Lewis, C. S., *The Four Loves*, New York, NY, Twenty-third Publications, 1985.

Lippmann, Walter, *A Preface to Morals*, New York, NY, Time-Life Books, 1929.

Maslin, Bonnie and Nir, Yehuda, *Not Quite Paradise*, Garden City, NY, Doubleday, 1987.

May, Rollo, *Love and Will*, New York, NY, W. W. Norton & Co., 1969.

May, Rollo, *Power and Innocence: A Search for the Sources of Violence*, New York, NY, W.W. Norton and Company, 1972.

McDonough, Yona Zeldis, *Tying the Knot*, New York, NY, Penguin Books, 1990.

Menninger, Karl A., *Whatever Became of Sin?*, New York, NY, Hawthorn Books, 1973.

Miles, Rosalind, *Love, Sex, Death and the Making of the Male*, New York, NY, Simon & Schuster, 1991.

Mills, C. Wright, *The Power Elite*, New York, NY, Oxford University Press, 1956.

Nash, Ogden, *I Wouldn't Have Missed It,* Boston, MA, Little, Brown & Co., 1975.

Neely, Dr. James C., *Gender*, New York, NY, Simon & Schuster, 1981.

Nelson, James B., *Embodiment*, Minneapolis, MN, Augsburg Publishing, 1978.

Ochs, Carol, *Behind the Sex of God*, Boston, MA, Beacon Press, 1977.

Olthuis, James H., *I Pledge You My Troth*, New York, NY, Harper and Row, 1975.

O'Neill, George and Nena, *Open Marriage: A New Lifestyle For Couples,* New York, NY, M. Evans and Company, Inc., 1972.

Pearsall, Paul, Ph.D., *The Power of the Family*, New York, NY, Doubleday, 1990.

Peck, M. Scott, *The Road Less Traveled*, New York, NY, Simon & Schuster, 1978.

Pike, James A., *If You Marry Outside Your Faith*, New York, NY, Harper & Brothers, 1954.

Powell, John, *The Secret of Staying in Love*, Niles, IL, Argus Communications, 1974.

Reich, *The Greening of America*, New York, NY, Random House, 1970.

Riesman, David, *The Lonely Crowd,* New Haven, CT, Yale University Press, 1950.

Rogers, Carl R., *Becoming Partners: Marriage and Its Alternatives*, New York, NY, Delacorte Press, 1972.

Ruben, Dr. Harvey L., *Supermarriage*, New York, NY, Bantam Books, 1986

Russell, Bertrand, *Marriage and Morals*, New York, NY, Liveright Publishing, 1929.

Scarf, Maggie, *Intimate Partners: Patterns In Love and Marriage*, New York, NY, Random House, 1987.

Schuller, Robert H., *Self Esteem: The New Reformation*, Waco, TX, Word Books, 1982.

Scroggs, Robin, *The New Testament and Homosexuality*, Philadelphia, PA, Fortress, 1983.

Shapiro, Stephen A., *Manhood: A New Definition*, New York, NY, G. P. Putnam's Sons, 1984.

Sheen, Fulton J., *Three To Get Married*, New York, NY, Dell Publishing Company, Inc., 1951.

Slater, Philip E., *The Pursuit of Loneliness: American Culture at the Breaking Point*, Boston, MA, Beacon Press, 1970.

Smedes, Lewis B., *Love Within Limits*, Grand Rapids, MI, William B. Eerdmans Publishing, 1978.

Smedes, Lewis B., *Sex for Christians*, Grand Rapids, MI, William B. Eerdmans Publishing, 1976.

Spong, John Shelby, *Living in Sin?*, San Francisco, CA, Harper & Row, 1988.

Tannahill, Reay, *Sex In History*, New York, NY, Stein & Day, 1980.

Tournier, Paul, *To Understand Each Other*, Richmond, VA, John Knox Press, 1967.

Weiner-Davis, Michele, *Divorce Busting*, New York, NY, Simon and Schuster, 1992.

Williams, Daniel Day, *The Spirit and the Forms of Love*, New York, NY, Harper & Row, 1968.

Winter, Gibson, *Love and Conflict*, Garden City, NY, Doubleday, 1958.

Wylie, W.P., *Human Nature and Christian Marriage*, Naperville, IL, SCM Press, Ltd., 1958.